Mountain Bike Maintenance

Mountain Bike Maintenance

Peter Ballin

THE CROWOOD PRESS

First published in 2017 by
The Crowood Press Ltd
Ramsbury, Marlborough
Wiltshire SN8 2HR

www.crowood.com

British Library Cataloguing-in-Publication Data
A catalogue record for this book is available from the British Library.

ISBN 978 178500 332 5

Typeset by Sharon Dainton
Printed and bound in India by Parksons Graphics

CONTENTS

CONTENTS

CHAPTER I

EVOLUTION OF THE BIKE

1817 – The Walking Machine

Initially developed as an alternative to travel by horse, a German named Karl Drais invented the first practical bicycle, which he named the Draisine. It was powered by scooting and, due to its solid wooden wheels and frame, it was incredibly uncomfortable on anything but the smoothest of terrain and hence struggled to gain popularity.

The walking machine.

1865 – The Velocipede

In 1865 the next generation of bicycle appeared, this time with pedals mounted to the front wheel. It was named Velocipede, Latin for 'fast foot', and was nicknamed The Boneshaker. Its wooden frame and metal tyres, combined with the cobbled streets of the day, again made for an extremely uncomfortable ride.

1870 – The Penny Farthing

Thanks to advancements in alloys, the first metal-framed bicycle appeared in around 1870. The high-wheel bicycle was the obvious next step from the Velocipede; the large front wheel enabled faster speeds and also gave a smoother ride, assisted by metal spokes and rubber tyres. The design quickly became very popular, but also gained a reputation for being dangerous due to the rider sitting so high. The iconic Penny Farthing is the most famous of the high-wheel bicycles.

The Velocipede.

The high-wheel bicycle.

The safety bicycle.

US Army bicycle.

Early cyclo-cross bike.

Klunker.

A mountain bike from the 1980s.

1880 – The Safety Bicycle

Bearing many similarities to a modern bike, the safety bicycle was a big turning point in the bicycle's evolution. Locating a chain-drive transmission between the two wheels helped to increase stability. This was one of the most important differences between the safety bicycle and its ancestors – it made people see the bicycle as a legitimate means of transport, no longer a dangerous toy.

The Birth of the Modern Mountain Bike

In 1896 the US Army introduced the first specifically modified off-road bicycle to replace horses. As bicycles don't need food, water or rest, cannot become ill and, most importantly, are not easily killed, it was an obvious choice to replace the costly horse. The first modified off-road bicycles were all built with rigid frames and forks.

Less than a decade later, in 1902, European road racers founded the road cycling-based sport of cyclo-cross. During organized road races, riders would take short cuts through farmers' fields to get to the next town quicker. The idea stuck and cyclo-cross was born. The invention of the sport is the first recorded instance of bicycles being raced off-road.

In 1955 a group of cyclists from the United Kingdom created The Rough Stuff Fellowship, a club for cyclists that wanted to ride off-road.

In the early 1970s a group of riders from California retrofitted a heavy beach cruiser from the 1930s with fat balloon tyres, better brakes and motocross handlebars. These bikes became known as Klunkers and were used to race down mountain fire roads. As these races become bigger they became known as Repack races, due to the grease in the hub brakes heating up so much it would melt and spill out, requiring the rider to repack their hubs after each run. Repack racing rapidly became popular and more competitive, sparking innovation for some of the first ever specially designed mountain bike products.

In the late 1970s, leading into the early 1980s, a few road bike companies started to mass produce the first mountain bikes, which to begin with were seen as a short-term fad. The first mass-produced mountain bikes were modified road bike frames that had thicker tubing for strength, wider tyre clearance for the larger tyres, and the first flat handlebars to give better stability. Until the late 1980s the sport of mountain biking was still in its infancy and therefore was not taken seriously by the larger bike brands.

In the late 1980s and early 1990s the popularity of mountain biking rapidly grew due to recognition from the media. There were televised events and athletes with big sponsorship deals, which in turn increased innovation in mountain bike technology. People started to realize the benefits of an all-terrain bicycle and larger bicycle manufacturers started to produce mountain bikes (MTB) and invest in new technology.

The Different Types of Mountain Bike

The limits of mountain bike performance and rider skill are constantly being pushed. Whether it's riding longer distances, getting down a mountain faster, jumping bigger gaps or hopping between obstacles more quickly or with more style, the progression of the sport is in constant flux. Due to these different specializations, mountain biking has branched off into multiple unique disciplines, with each requiring its own specific bike and equipment. Manufacturers and competitors are always looking for an edge over the competition, so constant technological and manufacturing development is achieved and new technologies are often quickly transferred from one discipline to another.

Modern mountain biking can be roughly split between these eight disciplines.

Cross-country (XC)
Cross-country is the most common mountain bike discipline and is currently the only one that is also an Olympic sport. It usually involves a mass or interval start, with riders racing a long, often looped, track. The tracks tend to be of a lower technical skill level and the focus is more on fitness and endurance. Tracks are made up of many climbs and descents across a mixture of terrain: loamy forest single tracks, gravelly

A mountain bike from the 1990s.

fire roads and even tarmac sections between off-road stages. Owing to the difficulty in televising an XC race and the low frequency of jumps and crashes, cross-country has a small viewing audience despite having a greater professional and amateur competitive turnout than any of the other disciplines.

Cross-country bikes can be either hardtails or short travel, full suspension bikes. A hardtail allows a more efficient power transfer, whereas a small amount of rear suspension allows the rider to traverse rougher sections faster but he or she may lose some of the power of a pedal stroke to the action of the suspension.

The steep geometry of a cross-country bike is designed to put the rider in an upright position for riding, making climbing a lot easier as well as allowing easier steering at lower speeds.

Trail/Enduro
Trail biking is the bridge between downhill and cross-country; in essence it is what mountain biking is all

Cross-country bike.

All-mountain bike.

Downhill bike.

Freeride bike.

about. Trail bikes are often hailed as 'do anything' or 'one bikes', as in one bike to do it all.

All-mountain bikes are for riders who want to ride to the top of the trail, but still want to ride at speed and tackle technical sections, jumps and drops on the descent. From this concept, the MTB race discipline of enduro was born. This involves multiple timed downhill stages with riders having to pedal, often uphill, between stages. A trail bike features front and rear suspension with 140–180mm of travel. The bikes are required to be lightweight for the climbs but also tough enough to be able to cope with rough terrain, drops and jumps on the descents. The geometry on an AM bike is considerably slacker in comparison to an XC bike, meaning the angle of the front forks is more relaxed and the bike has a longer wheelbase. This makes the bike more stable and easier to control on the descent and at high speed.

Downhill (DH)

Downhill mountain biking is exclusively, as the name suggests, a downhill sport. Riders are transported to the top of the hill by means of a vehicle or ski lift, often referred to as an uplift.

Downhill trails are far more technical than those used in other forms of mountain biking. They feature drops, jumps and incredibly rough terrain, and are often made up of large areas of mud, rocks or roots.

The extreme nature of downhill trails is made easier to tackle by the large amount of suspension of downhill bikes – around 200mm of travel – along with thick, dual ply tyres and very slack geometry, putting the rider in the right position to tackle these obstacles as well as making the bike a lot more stable at the higher speeds associated with downhill.

Freeride (FR)

Stemming from downhill but lacking the timed aspect, freeride is all about style and tricks. The bikes are almost indistinguishable from downhill race bikes but the aim is for the rider to demonstrate his or her skill over a series of large jumps and drops. Tricks can involve spinning the bike around the horizontal or vertical axis and removing appendages from the bike in mid-air.

Dual Slalom (DS)

Dual slalom involves two riders competing head-to-head down two identical trails that run parallel to one another. The concept itself came originally from dual slalom ski racing. DS was a Mountain Bike World Cup discipline for many years until it was replaced by four-cross in the early 2000s. Despite its removal from the World Cup tour it is still a popular discipline and a crowd favourite at events such as Crankworx and the Sea Otter Classic.

Dual slalom bikes are predominantly lightweight hardtails, however short travel, full suspension is also common. The bikes are tough, with short wheelbases allowing fast turning and quick acceleration.

Four-cross (4X)

4X is derived from BMX racing, with four riders competing head-to-head down a wide track of jumps and berms. The difference between 4X and BMX racetracks is that 4X tracks are predominantly downhill and can feature drops, rocks and roots alongside the large BMX-style jumps. The bikes used in 4X racing are almost indistinguishable from those used in dual slalom.

Trials

Mountain bike trials follow the same principles as motorbike trials. The rider has to negotiate a route through natural or man-made obstacles without putting his or her feet down or falling off. The racing is slow and technical, with riders achieving the summits of large obstacles with a series of hops on either wheels or just the rear wheel. In a trials competition, if any part of the rider or the bike except the tyres touch the course the rider will be given a point. The winner is the rider who completes the course with the fewest points.

Trials bikes feature no suspension at all, small gear ratios and long stems. They are available with mountain bike-style 26in, or much smaller 20in, wheels.

Dual slalom bike.

Fat Bike

Fat bikes have oversize tyres, enabling the rider to ride on soft terrain where normal mountain bikes would get stuck. These high volume, wide tyres can be ridden on snow, sand and wet boggy ground. The tyres are designed to be ridden at low pressure (8–10psi) which acts like suspension, giving a smooth ride over rougher terrain.

Fat bike.

CHAPTER 2

LEARNING THE PARTS OF A MOUNTAIN BIKE

The Parts of a Mountain Bike

While riding, servicing or repairing mountain bikes, it's vital to know the names for the different parts. This will be useful when ordering replacements or trying to explain to a bike shop a problem you may be having with your bike.

Frame

The frame is the main structure of the bike to which the majority of the components attach. A frame can be made of aluminium, steel or carbon fibre. By varying the type of material, the shape and size of the tubing, and the angles between each piece, a manufacturer can achieve many different properties from a frame. The primary concerns for frame manufacture are strength and weight. But head-angle, wheelbase, rear suspension position and type of suspension linkage are all key factors in building a frame that will excel in its destined discipline.

Forks

The forks are the part of the bike that attaches the front wheel to the frame. Nearly all mountain bikes feature a suspension fork these days. Front suspension helps absorb the bumps and give a smoother ride, saving riders energy and allowing them to ride faster and for longer.

The parts of a mountain bike.

Rear Shock

On a full suspension bike, the rear shock sits between the front and rear triangle of the bike's frame. Its job is to absorb bumps, increase grip and give the rider better control.

Headset

The headset is the set of bearings at the front of the bike that attaches the forks to the frame and, if adjusted correctly, will allow smooth steering. The bearings sit in two cups, upper and lower, and are held in compression by a top cap and star-fangled nut.

Handlebars

The handlebars are the main contact point at the front of the bike; they help with steering, stability and also offer a convenient mounting place for brake levers and shifters. Bars are available in various materials, lengths and heights, and with different degrees of sweep.

Stem

The stem connects the handlebars to the forks, allowing you to steer the bike. A longer stem will make steering less responsive but will help the rider get his or her weight forward, which will be good for climbs. A shorter stem will make the steering more responsive and will help the rider get his or her weight back for steep descents.

Brake Levers

The brake levers are located on the handlebars and should be within easy reach of the hands. They allow the rider to either modulate their speed or stop the bike completely. This is achieved by transmitting a rider's applied braking through to the brake calipers – either by a steel cable or hydraulic fluid.

Grips

The grips are the point where the hands contact the bike; their purpose is to give the rider's hands a surface to 'grip' whilst reducing vibration transmitted to the rider. If you find you have sore hands after riding it's worth experimenting with different thicknesses and compounds of grip. Typically larger hands prefer a larger diameter grip but this may not always be the case.

Gear Shifters

The shifters are normally located next to the grips; they allow the rider to change gear without removing his or her hands.

Tyres

Tyre choice is critical, they are the only part of the bike that makes contact with the ground. A tyre needs to be able to transmit power from the pedals whilst providing grip for cornering and braking. Tyre manufacturers produce many types of tyre for each cycling discipline. XC tyres need to be light and have very little rolling resistance. A downhill or freeride tyre needs to have good cornering and braking grip whilst possessing great puncture resistance. Each discipline will have tyre options for wet and dry conditions.

Rim

The rim is the aluminium or carbon fibre hoop into which the tyre sits and the spokes are threaded. Older or more basic bicycles may use the rim as a braking surface when using V or cantilever brakes.

Hub

The hub is the centre of the wheel; it consists of the hub shell, axle and bearing. The shell has two metal flanges where the spokes attach, holes drilled to mount a disc brake rotor, and a rear hub will feature a freehub. A ratchet mechanism inside the freehub allows the cassette to freewheel whilst the bike is rolling but engage when power is applied through the drivetrain.

Spokes

The spokes are threaded metal rods that attach the hub to the rim. Each spoke threads into a threaded cylinder called a nipple. Spokes are held under tension and this is where the wheel gets its strength. By adjusting the tension of each nipple a wheel can be straightened or made 'true'.

Disc Rotor

The brake rotors are a flat steel or aluminium disc that attaches to the centre of the hub to provide a braking surface for the brake caliper. Rotors often feature elaborate patterns, and have drilled holes to allow heat to dissipate and debris or dirt to clear. Cross-country and lighter applications will use a smaller disc, as less braking force is required. Downhill bikes tend to feature the largest size available, 203mm, for the ultimate in braking performance.

Brake Caliper

The brake caliper is the housing for the brake pads and pistons. These apply the braking force to the disc brake rotor via hydraulic pressure applied with the brake lever.

Pedals

The pedals are the main contact point for the feet. They provide a stable surface for the rider to stand on and allow pressure to be exerted to power the bike.

Cranks

The cranks connect the pedals to the drivetrain. They support the rider's weight and allow him or her to achieve the pedalling motion. The cranks are mounted to the bike via a bottom bracket, threaded cups containing bearings that support the cranks axel.

Chainring

The chainring is the main gear cog that allows power transfer from the cranks to the rear wheel. Depending on use, chainring sizes can vary from forty-four or more teeth down to around twenty-eight for most mountain bike applications. Trials bikes may feature even smaller-sized chainrings to achieve higher gear ratios.

A recent development in drivetrain technology is 'narrow-wide'.

A narrow-wide chainring features alternative narrow and wide teeth. These mesh with the narrow and wider links on a chain, creating a much better fit and eliminating lateral movement of the chain. This leads to a much improved ability to keep the chain on the chainring and almost completely eliminates the need for a chain guide when paired with a clutched mech.

Cassette

The cassette is the stack of cogs mounted to the rear wheel, they work with the rear derailleur to provide the rider with choice of gears. Usually the stack consists of around ten cogs, but some modern CX bikes can have up to twelve. The cog sizes range from as little as eleven teeth all the way up to as many as forty teeth, allowing for a large range of gear ratio options with only a single front chainring.

The larger the cog on the cassette the easier it will be to be pedal uphill.

Rear Derailleur

The rear derailleur, also known as a rear mech, is the heart of the drivetrain and also its most complex component. Its job is to move the chain across the cassette when the rider selects a gear. When the rear shifter is operated, tension is either applied or released to the gear cable. This tension is translated as lateral movement by the derailleur, which in turn pushes or pulls the chain into the required gear. The rear derailleur also acts as a chain tensioner, keeping the chain under tension through different size gears. Modern mountain bike derailleurs often have a clutch system, keeping the chain under tension at all times and helping to prevent the chain falling off the chainring over rough terrain.

Chain

The job of the chain is to transfer power from the pedals to the rear wheel, propelling the bike forward. Chains vary only in their width, which is specific to the amount of gears on the cassette. Chains tend to then come in eight-, nine-, ten- and eleven-speed varieties.

Seatpost/Dropper Seatpost

The seatpost connects the saddle to the frame. You can normally adjust the height by loosening off the seatpost clamp, positioning the saddle where preferred and then retightening the seatpost clamp. Dropper seatposts allow the rider to remotely adjust the seat height while riding. This is by means of hydraulic or cable-activated lever, which is mounted on the handlebars, and allows the saddle to be dropped out of the way for technical descents or raised to improve pedalling efficiency when climbing.

Saddle

The saddle is the third contact point between rider

and bike. It provides a place to sit and also helps the rider keep control of the bike in turns by applying sideways pressure with his or her inner thigh.

Chain Guide

Also known as chain device. The job of a chain guide is to stop the chain from coming off the chainring over bumpy terrain. There are many varieties of chain device on the market, most employ either plastic sliders or small toothed wheels to keep the chain in place.

Riding Gear

Safety First

No matter whether you're a novice or a seasoned professional, falling off your bike is all part of mountain biking. So it's important to minimize the risk of injury by using the correct protective equipment. Wearing good protective gear is often the difference between getting up and dusting yourself off, or having your day's riding ended by a crash.

Helmet

Remember to always wear a helmet while riding your bike, no exceptions! Helmets save lives and seriously reduce the severity of head injuries. There are two main types of helmet: the half-face and the full-face. Half-face helmets are intended for cross-country and all mountain use; they are designed to be lightweight while offering adequate protection from side and rear impacts.

Full-face helmets are intended to help protect the whole of your head for the more extreme disciplines of mountain biking. The mouthpiece of the helmet protects the face whilst the improved structural integrity provides extra protection for the skull.

Bear in mind, whatever type of helmet you use it needs to fit correctly. It should have a good snug fit with no movement when shaken around. If you have a crash it is very important to check the helmet for damage; it is also good practice to do this on a regular basis even if you haven't crashed. If the helmet has any cracks it is important to replace it immediately as it will no longer be 100 per cent effective in the event of a crash.

Gloves

Using gloves is important to help protect your hands as when you fall off your bike, the most natural thing to do is put your hands out. Gloves also provide you with more grip, especially in wet conditions, and can greatly reduce hand pain.

HELMETS

EYEWEAR

GLOVES

BODY ARMOUR

SHORTS

MTB SPECIFIC SHOES

KNEE AND ELBOW PADS

Riding gear and protective equipment.

Shorts

There are different types of mountain bike shorts; shorts that are designed for endurance that often have built-in Lycra to reduce chaffing on long rides, and shorts that have built-in padding for protection, which is ideal for disciplines such as downhill and freeride.

Knees and Elbows

The knees and elbows are some of the most vulnerable parts of the body.

If you're riding anything more technically challenging than light cross-country it's worth using a set of knee and elbow pads to reduce the risk of cuts, bruises or worse.

Shoes

Using the right shoes for mountain biking is important as they give you more grip, which gives you better control of the bike. Mountain bike shoes are normally made out of tough materials, helping improve pedalling efficiency and protect your feet against impacts. Some riders like to use shoes that clip into a corresponding pedal via a metal cleat attracted to the underside of the shoe, these pedals are known as 'clipless pedals'. Clipless pedals help improve pedalling efficiency, and keep your feet securely in place over the rough bumps. These types of pedal are not recommended for novice riders as they can be hard to master the technique of getting in and out of.

Eyewear

Having good eyewear is important to protect your eyes from mud and debris thrown up off your tyres. For cross-country with a half face helmet it's worth using wrap around, anti-fog glasses, which quite often come with selection of lenses for different light conditions. When it comes to riding more extreme terrain, normally with a full-face helmet it is better to use goggles.

Goggles offer a wider frame of vision, help keep your helmet secure and offer increased eye protection.

Body Armour and Neck Protection

For disciplines of mountain biking where high-speed crashes are likely, neck and back protection is recommended.

The most effective upper body protection is the full jacket, offering protection for the back, chest, shoulders, elbows and forearms. This type of upper body protection is ideal for users new to DH and AM. The drawback is they can be restrictive and very hot during summer months.

Spine or back protectors are a lightened version of the full jacket. Without the arm and chest protection, a back protector is much lighter and cooler than a full jacket whist still offering great spinal protection. There are a number of different backpacks that have built-in back protection; these are ideal for occasional riders, people who prefer to ride with a backpack and enduro racers.

Neck braces can be expensive, and most should only be worn with a full-face helmet. The neck brace works with the helmet restricting the movement of your neck during a crash, reducing the risk of injury.

CHAPTER 3

BASIC RIDING TECHNIQUES

This section of the book is to give you a brief insight into some basic mountain bike skills, helping you to have more fun and stay safe on the bike. Remember, it's always worth taking time to learn new skills, so you can build confidence and give yourself a solid platform to grow upon. As your riding ability starts to improve, the way you set up and maintain your bike will evolve to complement your new riding style. People start to favour one-finger braking, adjusting things such as handlebar position and suspension set-up to help them get the most out of their bike.

Attack Position

The attack position is one of the primarily skills for any mountain biker. It helps improve stability, turning and puts you in the correct position to react to challenging obstacles. To practice the attack position, rest the bike against a wall or ask a friend to hold your bike stable for you.

Step 1: Stand up on the bike while keeping the pedals level; try to have around 60 per cent of your weight over the pedals.

Step 2: Stand with your elbows bent directly above the handlebars, placing the other 40 per cent of your weight over the grips. This will help the front wheel to grip in turn and give you a solid position on the bike.

Step 3: Keep your knees away from the frame; try to have them run parallel with your pedals. This will help improve balance and give more space when turning.

Step 4: Keep your arms and knees slightly bent to help absorb bumps.

The attack position.

Look Ahead

One of the simplest but most effective ways to improve your riding is to remember to keep looking ahead down the trail and not down at your front wheel. This will help you prepare for the terrain and avoid any nasty surprises. Remember, the faster you ride, the less stopping time you have, so you will need to look even further ahead down the trail.

Don't Fixate on Hazards

When you spot a hazard, a ditch or tree for example, look where you want to go and not at the hazard itself. Your bike will tend to follow the line of your

Riding a flat turn.

Riding a berm.

gaze, so if you're looking directly at a hazard, that's likely where you'll end up.

How To: Ride Flat Turns

Learning to corner well is all about carrying speed out of the turn, the better you can do this the smoother and faster you'll be able to ride. The basic principles are fairly simple and can be learned in no time, but can take a lifetime to master.

Step 1: Set up for the turn as high (towards the outside of the corner) as possible; this will give you more space to turn. Before you start to initiate the turn; look for the exit; this will help you take the best line through the turn and also help put your body in the right position. Remember, where you look, the bike follows.

Step 2: Make sure you have all your braking done before the turn. It's better to brake early and carry speed out of the turn than to panic brake in the middle of the turn and lose all your momentum. When possible, never brake in corners.

Step 3: Initiate the turn by leaning the bike between your legs. Do this by applying pressure to the outside pedal while leaning with your legs, trying to keeping your upper body central. The purpose of leaning the bike is to help the turning edge of the tyre dig into the ground, thus giving more grip.

Step 4: After you have initiated the turn, stay off the brakes, keep your weight over the front wheel and never take your eyes off the exit of the corner.

Step 5: To exit the corner, focus on the trail ahead, let the bike straighten up and naturally drift to the outside edge of the corner.

How To: Ride Berms

A berm is a bank of dirt that runs around the edge of the entire corner. Their purpose is to give more grip, allowing the rider to turn with little or no braking. Although you can ride berms a lot faster than flat corners, the speed will vary depending on the sharpness of the corner and the size of the berm.

Step 1: Start like you would for a flat corner and make

sure you have all your braking done before the berm.

Step 2: As you approach the entrance of the berm, stand up on the pedals with your feet level and make sure you have around 60 per cent of your weight over the front wheel, reducing the chance of it sliding out.

Step 3: Drop your inside shoulder while looking to the exit and let the bike flow around the berm.

For berms that are really tight or loose it may help to put all your weight on the outside pedal, which will help drive the tyre into the dirt. A good mantra to hold in your mind when practising berms is: Go in high, come out low.

How To: Climb

It does not matter how fit you are; refining your climbing technique will help you climb faster and use less energy. Climbing may not always be easy, but overcoming a challenging climb is very rewarding.

Step 1: Anticipate the climb by making sure your saddle is at the correct height; your knees should have a slight amount of bend when your feet are at their lowest point.

Step 2: Make sure you're in the right gear before you start the climb. Trying to power up a climb in a higher gear may be fast, but it will sap your energy quickly. Ideally you want to pick a lower gear with a higher cadence, this will help conserve energy and reduce lactic acid build-up.

Step 3: Try to remain seated while climbing, unless the climb gets very steep. Climbing while seated saves a lot of energy as the bike supports your body weight. If the climb gets steep and you find the front wheel starting to lift off the ground, slide your body weight forward on the saddle or, if that does not work, stand up over the handlebars.

Step 4: Look ahead. A lot of people forget to look ahead and get caught out on unexpected obstacles.

The climbing position.

The descending position.

So keep looking up the climb and try to look out for smoother lines with more grip.

Step 5: As long as the climb is not too technical remember to lock out or stiffen up your suspension. Soft suspension is brilliant for absorbing rough descents but makes climbing a lot harder than it needs to be.

How To: Ride Steep Descents

Riding steeper sections of trail can be intimidating at first. Remember not to panic and, if you're not sure, there is no shame in walking down and returning at a later date.

Step 1: Start by entering the steep section slowly. This will help you gain control and give you time to plan ahead.

Step 2: Slide your body weight off the back of the bike so your weight is over the rear hub. Try to keep your body centred over the bike, with your knees resting above the pedals not in towards the frame or pointing away from the frame.

Step 3: Keep your arms slightly bent; this will help you keep some weight over the front wheel so it does not lose control and skid out.

Step 4: Try to refrain from dragging your brakes on long descents; instead brake firmly on flatter or smoother sections of trail and let off the brakes to allow the bike skip over the rougher sections.

Step 5: As you reach the bottom of the steep section, keep looking ahead and move your body back into 'attack position' so you are ready for the trail ahead.

How To: Ride Roots

If you find roots challenging, don't worry, you're not alone. Most mountain bikers find them difficult, especially when wet. If you follow a few basic principles you will be able to build up the confidence to ride roots effortlessly.

Step 1: Start in the attack position; this will help keep you stable on the bike.

Step 2: Try to avoid braking on roots, it can cause the wheels to quickly slide from underneath you and possibly result in a crash. Instead, look for gaps in between the roots and try to do your braking there. If the bike starts to slide don't be tempted to panic brake, try to stay calm and keep looking ahead.

Step 3: Avoid the roots. When riding roots especially when wet, it's better to try to ride without touching them. If there are only one or two roots try and lift the front wheel over them or if you can bunny hop over them. However, if the trail is covered with them you will need to try to 'unweight' the bike, by pushing it into the ground before the roots and then letting it spring up while riding over the roots, allowing it to skip over the top of them. While riding longer sections you will need more speed to keep the bike unweighted for the whole section.

Sometimes you can't avoid riding over roots. In which case avoid hitting them at an angle and try to pick a line where you hit them square on, which will reducing the risk of sliding.

Riding roots.

CHAPTER 4

THE RIGHT TOOL FOR THE JOB

It is very important to use the right tool for the job, using the wrong tool can end up causing you even more problems than you started with. Most people build up their tool kit over time and obtain tools as and when required. Remember to always buy quality tools that will last you for years, they really do make the difference.

Below we have listed the top fifteen most common tools; these should cover most basic jobs you will encounter.

Fifteen Most Common Tools

Allen Keys
A full of set of metric Allen keys, with sizes ranging from 1.5, 2, 2.5, 3, 4, 5, 6, 8, 10 and 12mm. If you are just starting out then a fold up set of Allen keys will be sufficient.

Later on, when they have been superseded in your toolbox by a set with handles, the folding set can kept as a portable set for use when out riding or away from your toolbox.

Allen keys.

Screwdrivers
You will only really need one flathead screwdriver and one cross head screwdriver, both size No.2. However, a full set of screwdrivers is usually inexpensive and will be useful over time.

Screwdrivers.

Tyre Levers
A set of plastic tyre levers should be more than sufficient to remove almost any tyre when used correctly. Plastic levers will reduce the risk of damage to the rim or inner tube whilst fitting the tyre.

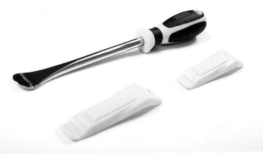

Tyre levers.

Spoke key.

Spanners.

Cassette tool and chain whip.   *Track pump.*

Cable cutters.   *Pliers.*

Chain tool.   *Torx keys.*

Spoke Key

The correct spoke key for your spoke nipples. The most common nipple sizes are: 127in (3.23mm), 130in (3.30mm) and 136in (3.45mm). Also note that some wheel manufacturers require specific spoke keys for their wheels.

Spanners

A full set of metric spanners ranging from 6mm to 26mm is ideal, but 6, 8, 9, 10, 15, 17 and 19mm are the most commonly used sizes and should cover most situations.

Cassette Tool and Chain Whip

If you need to remove your cassette, you will need a cassette tool and chain whip.

The socket-like cassette tool comes in two varieties, Shimano or Sram.

Track Pump

You will need a track pump with a pressure gauge. A decent track pump will inflate your tyres to the correct pressure with ease. A smaller hand pump that will fit in a backpack is recommended for use on the trail.

Cable Cutters

A quality set of cable cutters are important to ensure a clean cut while cutting inner cable and outer casing. Specialist hose cutters are available for hydraulic hose but a good set of cable cutters are more than capable. Some also have a feature for crushing crimps.

Pliers

You will need a pair of normal and long-nosed pliers.

Chain Tool

Chain tools are useful for removing or shortening chains. It's worth getting a good one otherwise you could easily damage an expensive chain.

Torx Keys

Torx keys are similar to Allen keys but have a star-shaped head. It's worth having a full set including: T5, T6, T7, T8, T9, T10, T15, T20, T25, T27, T30, T40 and T50. The two most commonly used ones are the T25, used for disc rotor bolts, and the T30, used for chainring bolts. Torx keys are growing in popularity with manufacturers and it is estimated all bolts on new bikes may change to them over the next decade.

Mallet

It's important to have a plastic- or rubber-head mallet. A metal hammer will damage delicate components.

Shock Pump

You will need a shock pump for setting up your suspension correctly. Make sure the pump is correctly installed before you start adjusting the pressure.

Pedal Spanner

A pedal spanner is a 15mm spanner that is thinner than normal ones so it can pass between the pedal and crank. It normally has a longer handle to give you extra leverage to help remove sticky pedals. Please note that some models of pedal require a 6mm or 8mm Allen key. Also, pedals have a reverse thread on the non-drive side.

Large Adjustable Spanner

You will need an adjustable spanner with jaws that open to a minimum of 30mm and that has a handle of at least 200mm. Constantly ensure the jaws are tightly closed on the nut and always pull against the stationary jaws of the spanner.

Mallet.

Shock pump.

Pedal spanner.

Large adjustable spanner.

Bike stand.

Comprehensive Tools Guide

As you start to progress and tackle more advanced repairs; you will require a wider range of tools. Below we have listed a fully comprehensive tool guide, explaining the purpose of any you may encounter.

Bike Stand

A bike stand is at the core of almost any bicycle service or repair task. A good stand should be stable, hold the bike still, have a good range of height adjustment and feature a rotating clamp to give you the option to grip different parts of the bike depending on the task you are undertaking. It's worth getting a good quality stand that will last you for years, as some budget models can be fragile and unstable.

For the duration of this book we are assuming everybody is using a bike stand. A stand allows better access to the bike, ensures it cannot fall over during vigorous work, and will save any back pain and posture problems associated with kneeling or squatting next to a bike that's either lying, or upside down, on the floor.

If you are not using a stand, if you are performing a trackside repair for example, please be aware our instructions are written for stand use and may have to be adapted.

Headset Press

A headset press is a tool used to accurately press in and align headset cups into the headtube of a frame. It is strongly advised you do not attempt to hit the cups

Headset press.

Headset removal tool.

Crown race installation tool.

Crown race removal tool.

in with a mallet, as it is very easy to damage the frame or misalign the cups. A headset press can also be used for installing press-fit bottom brackets.

Headset Removal Tool
This tool is simple but very effective for removing headset cups that are pressed into the frame's head tube. The tools can range in size from 1 inch, or $1^1/8$ inch to $1^1/2$ inch, depending on the size of head tube you are working on.

Crown Race Setting Tool
The crown race setting tool is used to press the crown race securely on to the bottom steer tube.

Crown Race Removal Tool
This tool is used to safety remove the crown race that is pressed on to the bottom of the steerer tube.

Torque Wrench
A torque wrench is designed to prevent over-tightening. Most components on a bike will have a specific torque setting, ensuring you tighten the components to the correct amount without the risk of causing damage. Too tight, and you may shear the bolt or damage the thread. Too loose, and you risk components coming loose or falling off mid-ride.

Derailleur Hanger Realignment Tool
Derailleur hangers are designed to bend or snap in order to protect your rear derailleur. Bent derailleur

Torque wrench.

Derailleur hanger tool.

hangers can cause all sorts of problems with your gears. This tool works well for realignment, but remember to be very careful when doing larger adjustments as the hanger can snap easily.

Wheel Jig/Truing Stand

A wheel-truing stand is used for truing or straightening wheels. It allows you to spin the wheel and pinpoint any areas that might be misaligned or bent.

Wheel jig.

Circlip Pliers

A circlip is a sprung-steel ring used to retain cylindrical internal components on things such as hubs, brakes and forks. You will ideally have a pair of circlip pliers that have different heads, allowing you to adapt to different circlips sizes and types.

Spoke Thread Cutter

There are many different types and sizes of wheel, therefore it can be hard to always find the correct size spokes you may need. A spoke cutter allows you cut a new thread after you have cut the spoke down to the correct size, allowing you to make almost any size of spoke.

Circlip pliers.   *Spoke thread cutter.*

Chain Stretch Tester

It's not much fun when your gears start to skip from cog to cog and one of the reasons for this could be a stretched chain. This simple tool allows you to check the amount of stretch and tells you if your chain needs to be replaced.

Chain stretch tester.

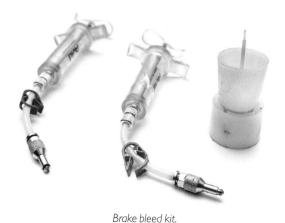

Brake bleed kit.

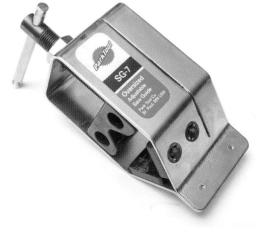

Hacksaw and saw guide.

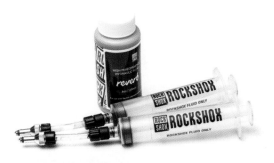

Reverb bleed kit.

Bleed Kit

When hydraulic brakes start to feel spongy or lose power during a descent, it's likely that they have air in the system. The best way to fix this problem is to bleed the brake. This involves using a bleed kit to change the oil and ensure there is no trapped air in the system.

Reverb Bleed Kit

Over time Avid Reverb dropper seatposts need to have the hydraulic fluid changed to keep them running smoothly. Never use a hydraulic brake bleed kit instead of the Reverb bleed kit because Reverbs use 2.5 weight oil and not Dot fluid, which would corrode the seals.

Socket Set

A complete metric socket set that includes: 6, 7, 8, 9, 10, 11, 12, 13, 14, 15, 16, 17, 18, 19, 20, 21, 22, 24, 27, 30 and 32mm. Sockets are handy for getting into tight areas and reduce damage to components or nuts/bolts as they have a larger contact area. They can also be used as a drift when pressing bearings in or out, if you don't have a bearing press.

Hacksaw and Saw Guide

You will need a good hacksaw for cutting down

Socket set.

seatposts, steerer tubes and handlebars. When cutting anything down remember to use a saw guide and always follow the measure twice, cut once rule. If you are cutting carbon fibre always use a fine 32 TPI blade and remember to use tape around the surface you are cutting to reduce splintering.

Vice
Vices are useful for many different jobs – from cutting things down to pressing bearings in. You will need a vice that has jaws that open to at least 150mm and it also needs to be securely mounted to a workshop bench.

Vice.

Vernier Calipers
Vernier calipers are an exceptionally accurate measuring tool, designed to be accurate up to 0.02mm. They are useful for when you need to replace very precise parts such as bearings, bushings and seals.

Cone Spanners
When loosening or tightening cup and cone bearings you will need to use cone spanners as they fit perfectly over the narrow flats of the cones while giving you enough leverage to ensure they are secure. A complete set of cone spanners range from 13, 14, 15, 16, 17, 18, 19, 20, 21, 22, 23, 24 and 28mm, but the most common sizes are 13, 15, 17 and 22mm.

Vernier calipers.

Bottom Bracket Tool
There are a number of different types of bottom bracket tool; the most common are the Shimano splined tool and the external bottom bracket tool. Remember; drive side loosens clockwise and non-driveside loosens anticlockwise. Always check the tool is correctly fitted before use.

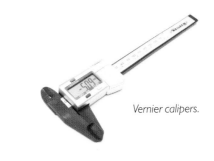

Cone spanners.   Bottom bracket tool.

Chainring Nut Tool
This tool's teeth slot into the back of the chainring bolt, preventing the nut from spinning while loosening or tightening.

Chasing and Facing Tools
The purpose of chasing and facing is to remove excess paint and metal from areas where components are mounted to the frame, namely the

Chainring nut tool.

Facing tool.

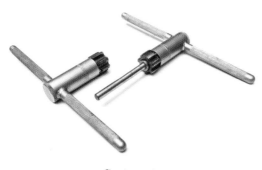

Chasing tool.

Star-nut setter.   *Spoke ruler.*

Wheel alignment gauge.   *Drill.*

bottom bracket, headtube and brake mounts. This process helps increase the longevity of components and also helps reduce frame noise, such as from creaking bottom brackets and headsets.

Star-Nut Setter

This tool makes it quick and easy to install star-fangled nuts into steerer tubes. Without this tool it can be a nightmare to get them in straight.

Spoke Ruler

Spoke rulers are important for ensuring you have the correct size spokes and most also have a ball bearing size gauge that can come in handy when replacing loose bearings in hubs and headsets.

Wheel Alignment Gauge

A wheel alignment gauge is also known as a dishing tool. Wheel dishing is the process of making sure the rim is centred correctly in the frame or forks. Having correctly dished wheels is important as an incorrectly dished one can cause the tyre to contact the frame, or make the bike unstable at speed.

Drill

A cordless drill can be handy for jobs such as unscrewing disc bolts or drilling out snapped frame bolts. Remember, when drilling ensure you are using the correct drill bit for drilling metal.

Dremel

Having a Dremel in your workshop is extremely useful, especially when it comes to removing snapped or rounded bolts.

Dremel.

Tap and Die Set

Tap and die sets are used for cutting new threads and are also useful for cleaning and recutting damaged threads. A tap cuts a thread into a hole (female thread) and a die cuts a thread on to a section of bar (male thread).

Easy-outs

Easy-outs are designed for removing broken or seized screws. First you need to drill a hole and then screw the reverse threaded easy-out into the hole; that should eventually release the seized screw. Remember, it's worth paying more for a better quality set, as cheaper units tend to fail quickly.

Axle Vice

An axle vice fits into your workshop vice and stops the axle from spinning while working on the hub.

Grease Gun

A grease gun is superb for keeping your hands clean and greasing tight areas such as hubs and grease ports.

Using a Torque Wrench

What is Torque?

Torque is the measurement of twisting force applied to an object that rotates, such as a bolt. To calculate torque (T) you multiply the Force (F) by the Length (L) of the lever on a rotational axis.

Torque is measured in Newton metres (Nm) or pound inches (lb-in).

Why Use a Torque Wrench?

Manufacturers are using a broader range of materials to make components lighter and these often become fragile when over-tightened or fitted incorrectly. This means it is more important than ever to ensure components are tightened to the correct tension. When you use a torque wrench you can be sure you're tightening the bolt up to the manufacturer's recommended tension.

If the tension is insufficient the component may come loose and the bolt will eventually rattle out and be lost. If the tension is too tight it will most likely

Tap and die set.

Easy-outs.

Axle vice.

Grease gun.

$$T = F \times L$$

Torque force diagram.

Beam wrench.

Digital wrench.

Click wrench.

cause damage to either the thread, the bolt or the component itself. Any of these could likely leave you with a big repair bill or cause an accident.

Different Types of Torque Wrenches

There are three main ones:

Beam Type

These wrenches have two beams, one of which points to a gauge that indicating the torque. If you notice the beam is not pointing to zero when not under tension, you can easily recalibrate it by simply bending the beam back to zero.

Click Type

The most common type of torque wrench. Click type wrenches need to be adjusted to the correct torque and then will click once the correct torque is achieved, thus ensuring you do not over-tighten.

Digital

The benefit of digital wrenches is they are accurate up to 2 per cent, unlike the click or beam wrenches that are usually only accurate to 3–5 per cent.

How To: Use a Torque Wrench

Don't be fooled into thinking you know how tight it needs to be. Even professional bike mechanics tend to think this, but after various experimental tests it was found that even they are not as accurate as they think.

Step 1: Find the correct torque setting that corresponds to the component you want to fasten. This will vary between different components and manufacturers, so check the user manual or manufacturer's website.

Step 2: Set the required torque setting either by twisting the adjuster on a click wrench or using the buttons on a digital wrench.

Step 3: Attach the appropriate driver; a socket, Allen key or Torx key.

Step 4: Fasten to the correct torque. With the beam wrench, stop when the bar indicates the correct torque, with a click wrench it should not allow you to over-tension and will start to click. With a digital wrench it will usually indicate with a green light to show you have reached the required torque.

Step 2: Using a torque wrench.

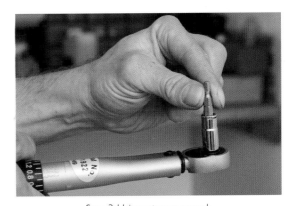

Step 3: Using a torque wrench.

TOP TIP

Never exceed the working range of the wrench. Always store in the hard case provided. If the wrench is in constant use, make sure it's recalibrated once a year by the manufacturer or a reputable servicer.

Step 4: Using a torque wrench .

31

Lubes overview.

Chain lube.

Bearing grease.

Carbon grease.

Lubes, Thread Lock and Degreasers

Using the correct cleaning and lubricant products will help keep your bike running smoothly and improve component lifespan. Your list of potions and lotions will start to grow as you start to tackle more advanced jobs.

Lubricants

Chain Lubricant

Remember, you should only apply chain lube to a clean chain. This is important because otherwise it will mix the new oil with dirt and create an oily grinding paste that will wear out your expensive chain and cassette in no time. In dry conditions you should use dry lubricant as it's thinner and therefore attracts less sand or dirt, reducing wear. Beware on longer rides, as you may need to reapply dry lubricant to avoid the chain running dry. In wet and muddy conditions wet lubricant works well because it's thick and sticky, which is ideal for staying on during harsh conditions.

TOP TIP

Chain lube is also a brilliant multi-use lubricant; it can be used on pivots, jockey wheels, gear cables, etc. It's recommended that a drip lubricant is used, as spray lubricants can easily contaminate braking surfaces.

Grease

Grease is a semi-solid, hard-wearing lubricant, most commonly used in sealed components such as hubs and headsets. This is to reduce the risk of water and dirt contamination, which will cause components to feel rough and accelerate wear. There are a number of different types of grease, so remember to use the correct grease for the appropriate application.

Bearing Grease

A tube of grease normally lasts quite a while, as most jobs don't require huge amounts, so it's worth investing in quality. If you're using a grease gun remember to make sure the grease-tube thread is compatible with your gun.

Carbon Fibre-Specific Grease

Normal grease can degrade the structure of carbon fibre; therefore while working on carbon components you should always use carbon-specific grease.

Anti-Seize Compound

Anti-seize compound is used to reduce friction and protect from corrosion on non-moving components. This includes seatposts, bottom bracket cups, pedal threads and press-fit components.

Anti-seize compound.   *Threadlock.*

Thread Lock

Thread lock is an adhesive compound that is used to stop threads from loosening; it usually comes in a number of different strengths depicted by colour. The most commonly used strength on mountain bikes is the medium strength, which is blue.

Degreasers

General Degreaser

A general degreaser is used to remove all the grease, muck and grime that builds up on a bicycle's moving parts. It is normally applied and agitated with a brush to help penetrate those hard-to-reach areas.

Disc Brake Cleaner

Disc brake cleaner is used to clean brake components of brake fluid and contaminants. It usually comes in spray form and is important to ensure you find an alcohol-based cleaner that will evaporate as otherwise it can leave a residue that can affect braking performance.

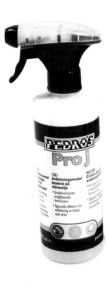

Degreaser.   *Disc brake cleaner.*

CHAPTER 5

BEFORE AND AFTER RIDING

Checking bike over.

Full bolt check.

Checking sag and rebound.

Pre-Ride Checks

Before you head out on your bike it's import to check it is safe to ride and is set up correctly. A few simple checks help avoid the long walk home or a potential injury.

Quick Bolt Check

Carefully work your way through the entire set of Allen keys and Torx bolts on the bike. Start at the back and move forward, checking every bolt is tight. Don't forget to check:

- Brake bolts (rotor bolts, caliper and frame-mounting bolts)
- Derailleur bolts including jockey wheel bolts
- Crank, chainring bolts and crank pinch bolts
- Frame pivot bolts and shock bolts
- Stem, headset, levers, grips and fork crown bolts
- Saddle and seatpost bolts
- Pedals

TOP TIP

To reduce the risk of over-tightening use a torque wrench. (See Chapter 4.)

Check Suspension is Set Up Correctly

- Inspect for damage to your forks and rear shock.
- Check for any leaks around the seals or any obvious signs of wear.
- Check the sag and the rebound (see Chapter 10: How To: Set Up Suspension).

Check Tyre Pressure

The correct tyre pressure should be printed on the sidewall of the tyre. If in doubt most mountain bike tyres should be pumped up to 30–35psi (2–2.5bar). After you have checked tyre pressure, inspect the tyre for any damage.

Check Your Gears are Set Up Correctly

Shift up and down through the gears, making sure the chain does not jump or skip. If you notice any problems and need to make any adjustments (*see* Chapter 8: How To: Index Gears)

Checking tyre pressure.

TOP TIP

Before checking the gears make sure the chain is clean and well lubricated.

Checking gears.

Check Your Brakes are Set Up Correctly

Check the brake lever is in the correct position. Check the lever does not feel spongy, if the lever feels spongy ensure the caliper is centred over the disc and make sure the brake pads have plenty of life left in them. If the brake still feels spongy you may need to bleed the brakes (*see* Chapter 9: How To: Bleed … Brakes).

Check the brake pads are not rubbing on the disc, if they are rubbing you will need to centre the brake caliper (*see* Chapter 9: How To: Align a Disc Brake Caliper) and also check to see if the disc is bent (see Chapter 9: How To: Straighten a Bent Disc Rotor). Check the brake hoses for any damage.

Checking brakes.

Check Spokes

Check the spokes are tight by running your hand around the wheel, gently pulling on each one. If you notice any loose spokes they will need to be tightened (*see* Chapter 6: How To: True a Wheel).

Checking spokes.

Say no to pressure washers!

Step 1: Remove loose dirt.

Step 2: Spray with a hose.

How To: Clean a Mountain Bike

After a long, wet and muddy ride all you want to do is throw your bike in the shed, jump in the shower and have a nice warm drink. Although this option might seem tempting you should try and clean your bike while the mud is still wet, otherwise the next time you come to use it it will be seized with rust and covered in hardened mud.

When a bike is left dirty for a period of time, the dirt in contact will absorb oil from components and bearings. This will lead to 'dry' components and accelerate wear.

Keeping your bike clean is one of the most important parts of mountain bike maintenance. It helps keep your bike functioning well and enables you to inspect for damaged or worn parts, which could potentially fail and be dangerous.

Say No to Pressure Washers

Be warned; when it comes to using a pressure washer on your bike, apart from making your bike clean and shiny they also push the grease out of sealed bearings. This will make them run dry and in turn will make bearings, pivots and seals wear faster; which will dramatically reduce the lifespan of your bike. If you are going to use a pressure washer, avoid bearings and greased components and keep the washer at least 1.5m from the bike.

Difficulty – 1/5
Time – 20 minutes

Tools
Brush set
Sponge
Rag
Hose
Parts
Bike cleaner spray
Chain lube
Polish (optional)

Step 1: Turn the bike upside down so it's resting on the saddle and handlebars. Scrape or knock off any large loose lumps of mud or dirt with a brush.

Step 2: Turn the hose on and lightly spray the whole bike. This is to help soften and remove the majority of the dirt. Pay attention to the hard-to-reach areas such as the back of the fork crown, the inside of the chainstay, hubs, cassette, brake calipers, and frame linkages.

Step 3: Spray the whole bike with bike cleaner. Pay extra attention to the grimy areas on the drivetrain. Try to avoid spraying the brake discs and calipers even if the product says it is OK, as some products can leave a residue that can affect braking performance. Leave the bike cleaner for three to five minutes.

Step 4: Take the largest brush and use it to remove any dirt or debris from all over the bike, then use the smaller brushes to get into the tighter areas such as the cassette, derailleur, brakes, etc. Re-apply bike cleaner to stubborn grime.

Step 5: Rinse off the bike cleaner with a hose, being careful not to use any pressure on sealed components such as fork seals, frame bearings, etc. Turn the bike upright and rest against a wall, or place in a bike stand. Repeat steps 3–5, making sure you did not miss anything. Leave bike to dry for fifteen minutes.

Step 6: Now degrease the drivetrain, paying attention to scrub the chain and cassette with degreaser. If possible use chain cleaner on the chain; it will make it look like new. Once done rinse off the drivetrain with fresh water.

Step 3: Spray with bike cleaner.

Step 4: Use brushes to loosen off dirt.

Step 5: Rinse off the cleaner with a hose.

37

Step 6: Degrease the drivetrain.

Step 7: Dry and apply lubricant.

Step 8: Polish with silicon spray.

TOP TIP

When cleaning your bike, it is a good time to inspect for damage, and check tyre and brake pad wear.

Step 7: Use a dry rag or old towel to ensure the chain is dry, and apply either wet or dry lubricant to the chain, depending on the riding conditions. Also add a drop of lubricant to each jockey wheel on the derailleur.

Step 8: Finish by using a silicon polish on everything apart from the brake discs and calipers. This will help protect the components, reduce friction on suspension and make your bike look new and shiny.

CHAPTER 6

WHEELS

Wheels are the key component of a bike, without them bicycles simply wouldn't exist. Because of their importance they are the first area we will cover in detail.

Wheel Size

Reinventing the Wheel
Historically, selecting the correct wheel size for a bike was never a problem as 26in wheels have been the industry standard since the early 1970s, going back to the time of the Californian Klunkers.

Over the interim years, manufacturers have experimented with different wheel sizes, although 26in wheels remained popular mainly due to the limited supply of wheels, tyres and spares in any other sizes.

In the end Gary Fisher, considered one of the pioneers of mountain biking, decided to use 29in wheels on his cross-country race bikes. He rightly believed the larger wheel size would give higher speeds and greater power transfer than the smaller 26in wheels, a clear advantage in XC racing. Although it must be noted that he was not the first person to attempt this, it was his influence that really started the 29in movement.

Unlike the other early 29in pioneers, it was his partnership with Trek Bicycles that helped to smooth initial problems with manufacturing and distribution.

After that, 29in began to grow in popularity, attracting more brands and in turn sparked a global trend towards bigger wheels for cross-country.

Recently the reign of the mighty 26in wheel in other disciplines has ended.

With 29in providing great rolling resistance, power transfer and stability, the question was raised if 26in was big enough for downhill, freeride and all-mountain use.

After several years of experimentation and disagreement, one clear winner from the wheel size arms race emerged: 650b or 27.5in was the perfect size

WHEEL SIZE COMPARISON

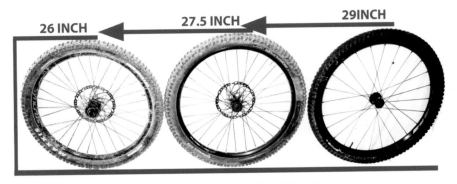

Size difference between 26in, 27.5in & 29in wheels.

between the acceleration and cornering ability of a 26in and the all-out power and rolling resistance of a 29in.

The 650b wheels were an instant success and quickly dominated the podiums at world-class downhill and enduro events.

What are the advantages and disadvantages of each wheel size?

26in Wheels

Advantages
Smaller lighter, more agile and accelerate faster.

26in wheels have been around for many years, making spares easy and cheap to come by. The smaller wheel size can be made stiffer and stronger than larger wheel sizes.

Disadvantages
Smaller wheels provide less contact with the ground, giving less grip, and can lead to twitchy steering and less stability at speed.

Smaller wheels can lose speed getting caught in holes that bigger wheels would easily roll through.

27.5in Wheels (650b)

Advantages
27.5in wheels give better handling than 29in wheels whilst still faster rolling than 26in wheels.

Unlike 29in wheels, they are still small enough to fit

An example of a 26in-wheeled bike suited to someone on a budget.

longer travel frames and forks without affecting rider position.

The larger tyre size noticeably improves grip and braking performance compared with 26in wheels.

Disadvantages
Finding spares such as inner tubes, tyres, spokes and rims can be harder compared with the traditional wheel sizes until shops replace their older 26in stock of spares.

29in Wheels

Advantages
29in wheels stall less on rough terrain, giving a more stable, smoother, faster ride and eliminate the need to for heavy long-travel suspension.

The larger wheels means the tyre has more contact with the ground, giving more grip and allowing the use of thinner, faster-rolling tyres.

For taller riders 29in wheels provide a bike that feels more in proportion to their size.

Disadvantages
The wheels are heavier and can be sluggish to get moving.

Larger wheels can make riding steep or slow twisty trails hard work.

Shorter riders may find the wheels cumbersome.

Which is the Right Wheel Size for You?

On a Budget
If you're on a tight budget the 26in wheel is the obvious choice. Most manufacturers are pushing bigger wheel sizes, meaning there is an abundance of cheap new and used 26in wheeled bikes.

Beginners and Less Confident Riders
If you are just getting into mountain biking or you are a less confident rider, 29in wheels could be the way forward as they give a smoother ride with more grip and stability.

Cross-country Rider/Racer
Whether you're a casual weekend cross-country rider or an international cross-country racer, 29in

An example of a 29in-wheeled bike suited to a beginner rider. (By scattata da F.Grifoni per conto di Laura Fortunato [Archila] via Wikimedia Commons)

An example of a 29in-wheeled bike suited to a cross-country rider. (By Steve Bennett via Wikimedia Commons)

An example of a 27.5in-wheeled bike suited to an enduro or downhill rider.

Differences in tyre widths.

Differences in sidewall thicknesses.

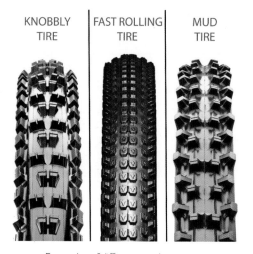

Examples of different tread patterns.

wheels are the only choice because of their ability to roll effortlessly through less technical trails and keep momentum.

Downhill, Enduro or Trail Riding
No matter what you ride, whether it is downhill, enduro or anything in between, 27.5in wheels seem to give the perfect balance of stability and agility, making them more versatile for most types of riding. Most manufacturers have stopped the production of 26in DH/AM frames. However, it's worth noting that 29in wheels are starting to gain popularity in these disciplines.

Tyre Choice

Having the correct tyres for the terrain and conditions that you are riding should never be underestimated. Bike tyres come in many different sizes and tread patterns. However, it can be the unseen details such as rubber compound, sidewall thickness, and tyre pressures that make a big difference to your riding.

Tyre Width
Firstly you need to select a tyre that fits the wheel size on your bike.

The tyre size is always stated on the sidewall of the tyre, so when replacing a tyre check the size of the old one. If building a new bike measure the rim diameter. Next you need to select an appropriate width of tyre. Most mountain bike tyres fall into a width range of 1.8in to 2.7in. Narrower tyres have less weight, and have less friction to overcome so are faster rolling. Wider tyres have a larger contact area with the ground helping to improve grip and stability.

Tyre Sidewall Plies
Tyre sidewalls are available in different thicknesses known as plies, either single ply or dual ply. Single ply sidewalls are thin and lightweight, ideal for disciplines such as cross-country where weight saving is important and less getting a puncture. Dual ply tyres are much sturdier and offer much better protection against punctures, however they are heavier and the rolling resistance is increased. Some manufacturers now offer single ply tyres combined with Kevlar sidewalls to help

prevent punctures whilst offering weight savings over dual ply tyres. Remember, different manufacturers have different names for single or dual ply, for example Michelin call dual ply tyres 'reinforced'.

Tread Pattern

When selecting a mountain bike tyre one of the main considerations should be the tread pattern. A knobbly tread provides better traction on loose terrain, also helping to give better control over roots and rocks. The downside to a knobbly tread is that it will not be best suited to trails that are hard and smooth. For these types of trail a tyre with low profile knobs will provide sufficient traction whilst offering lower rolling resistance. For muddy conditions a tyre with deep, widely spaced knobs and a narrow width will provide the best traction and mud clearance properties. Quite often it can be advantageous to run different tread patterns on the front and rear of the bike –the front tyre optimized for grip and the rear tyre optimized for rolling resistance.

Compound

Tyres are available in many different compounds of rubber. The softer the rubber compound, the more grip the rubber will give. However, a softer rubber compound will wear down faster and the tyre will not last as long as a harder compound rubber. Choosing a rubber compound will always be a trade-off between how much grip the tyre gives and how long the tyre will last. In recent years some tyre manufacturers have started to offer tyres with different rubber compounds on different areas of the tyre. This is because on a normal mountain bike tyre the centre part of the tread will wear faster than the outer edges as it spends more time in contact with the ground. A dual or triple compound tyre may be more expensive, but may be a worthwhile investment, as they can offer improved grip and better rolling, and last longer.

Tubeless

Some mountain bike tyres can be used without an inner tube. Running a tubeless system has the advantages of being lighter, and the ability to run lower pressures, with less risk of a pinch flat (as there is no inner tube to pinch). The disadvantages are that if you get a rip in the tyre, the tyre will lose pressure and will need to be repaired or fitted with a tube.

Examples of different compounds.

Tubeless tyre.

Schrader Valve.   *Presta Valve.*

A quick release axle (above) and a Maxle (below).

An axle with bolts.

A non-quick release Maxle.

Inner Tubes

Inner tubes can be found on hundreds of millions of vehicles worldwide. They were the key to the first successful pneumatic tyres and are one of the easiest components of a bike to replace. They are also one of the easiest to mess up during fitting.

Inner tubes are available in different weights for different applications. All inner tubes feature a valve to let air in and out in a controlled manner. These valves fall into two categories:

Schrader

The larger style of valve, also found on cars. Use a fingernail or a small object such as an Allen key to push in the valve core until all the air has been released.

Presta

Smaller and the most common valve used on bicycles. Unscrew the tip of valve two to three turns anticlockwise with your fingers, then gently press and hold down the valve tip until you have released all the air.

Types of Axle

Bike axles come in various shapes and sizes. The common theme throughout is they allow the removal of the bicycle's wheels quickly, cleanly and with the smallest amount of tools possible.

Quick Releases and Maxles

Quick releases undo by lifting the lever over the axle and unscrewing two to three turns. Maxles undo by lifting the lever and then placing the lever in the slot for the lever. Then fully unscrew the Maxle and pull away from the bike.

Axles with Bolts

Start by unscrewing the bolts three to four turns, most will have a built-in lock washer that grips to the frame and will need to be unhooked.

Non-Quick Release Maxle

Some forks such as RockShox Boxxers use a Maxle

that does not have a quick release lever. To remove this type of Maxle, loosen off one full turn the side of the Maxle that is flush is the fork lowers, then fully unscrew the other side of the Maxle and remove.

Bolt-Through Axle

First check the frame or fork lowers for pinch bolts that may be holding the axle secure. Undo pinch bolts one to two turns or until the bolt moves freely. Now unscrew the whole axle from the bolt located at the head of the axle. Most axles will unscrew with a metric spanner or an Allen key.

A bolt-through axle.

How To: Fit a Tyre

When working on or riding a bike it is often a requirement to remove a tyre.

Some will come off easily, and some will need a little more persuasion.

Changing a tyre is a basic skill that all bikers should learn as you don't want to be left stranded with a puncture in the middle of nowhere.

Difficulty – 2/5
Time – 10 minutes

Tools
Tyre levers
Pump

Step 1: Check the rim to make sure the rim tape is in place, and there are no sharp objects that could cause a puncture. For more on how to remove a tyre, *see* Chapter 6.

Step 2: Check the tyre to make sure it is free from thorns, glass and other debris.

Step 3: Inflate the inner tube so it has just enough air to hold its own shape.

Step 4: Check the direction arrow on the tyre and work one side on to the rim. If it's too tight to fit with your hands, use a tyre lever to get the final part over the rim.

Step 1: Check the rim.

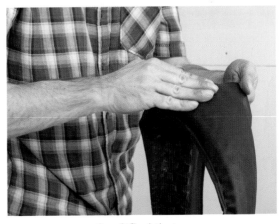

Step 2: Check the tyre.

Step 3: Inflate the inner tube.

Step 4: Fit the first side of the tyre to the rim.

Step 5: Fit the inner tube, and then finish fitting the tyre to the rim.

Step 5: Insert the tube into the tyre, placing the inner tube valve through the valve hole in the rim. Once the tube is fully inside the tyre, start to work the tyre bead on to the rim. It is best to start at the valve area and work your way around. If the bead is really stiff go back to the valve area and push the bead of the tyre into the rim.

If necessary use the tyre levers to pop the tyre on to the rim.

Step 6: Check that the inner tube isn't caught under the bead of the tyre. Squeeze the tyre and look down into the rim, checking all the way around on both sides of the tyre.

Step 7: Inflate the inner tube to the desired pressure. Most tyre manufacturers recommend 25–60psi depending on application, and mountain bikes tend to fall in the 30–35psi range; check the information shown on the sidewall of the tyre. Lower pressures will give more grip and provide a cushioning to your ride, but will be more prone to pinch punctures. Higher-pressure tyres will roll faster and will be less likely to puncture, but it will be a harsher ride and give lower levels of grip.

Step 6: Check the inner tube is not caught in the tyre.

Step 7: Inflate the tyre to the correct pressure.

How To: Fit a Tubeless Tyre

If you are looking for the ultimate in performance then tubeless tyres are the way to go, and if done correctly they are simple to fit. Just remember it's always worth carrying a spare tube in case the tyre gets damaged.

Difficulty – 3/5
Time – 10 minutes

Tools
Tyre lever
Pump (Track pump or compressor recommended)

Parts
Tubeless sealant

Step 1: Install the tubeless rim tape, ensure it is placed evenly on the rim and that it goes up the sides of the rim to form an airtight seal.

Step 2: Mount one side of the tyre on the rim. Using a sponge or paintbrush, coat both tyre beads in soapy water. This helps lubricate the tyre and allows it to slide into place on the rim more easily. If you have a tyre marked 'UST' you have a fully compatible tubeless tyre and should not need to use any sealant. If your tyre is marked 'tubeless ready' then tubeless sealant is needed to help seal the tyre and stop air leaking out of the rubber.

Step 3: If needed, pour the manufacturer's recommended amount of tubeless sealant into the tyre. Now mount the other bead of the tyre to the rim, using tyre levers if you can't fit the bead to the rim by hand.

Step 4: Rotate the tyre and shake to spread the tubeless sealant around the tyre.

Step 5: Inflate the tyre until the bead pops on to the rim. It's best to use a high-pressure pump or compressor to inflate the tyre, as it's necessary to quickly put a large volume of air into the tyre to force the bead into the rim. If using a hand pump, rapid pumping will be necessary. Be sure to not go over the

Step 1: Fit tubeless rim tape.

Step 2: Coat tyre bead with soapy water.

Step 3: Fit the tubeless tyre.

Step 4: Add sealant and fit the tyre to the rim.

tyre's maximum inflation pressure as stated on the sidewall. Now that the bead is seated on the rim you can let some air out to run the tyre at your desired pressure.

Step 5: Shake and rotate the tyre to spread the sealant.

Punctures

Sadly, you can't ride bikes without having the odd puncture, but with a little practice fixing punctures is simple and will most likely save you a long walk home.

Types of Puncture

Impact punctures are normally caused by sharp objects such as nails, thorns or sharp rocks that penetrate the tyre. Tiny punctures caused by thorns can take days to go down (known as a 'slow punctures'), while a major sidewall impact caused by a jagged rock can make a loud bang and deflate instantly.

Pinch punctures occur when you hit a sharp object and the inner tube is pinched against the rim. This type of puncture usually leaves two holes on either side of the tube, hence why it's also commonly known as a Snakebite. Snakebites are notoriously hard to repair with a puncture repair kit and a new inner tube is almost always required.

Spoke-related punctures result from the end of the spoke poking through the rim tape, puncturing the inner tube, and they occur relatively rarely.

How To: Fix a Puncture

The procedure for fixing a puncture is something every mountain biker should learn. You can carry a spare tube, but if you're having a bad day and you run out, a puncture repair kit can help prevent you from being stranded. With a little practice fixing punctures

Flat tyre due to a puncture.

An impact puncture.

A pinch puncture.

A spoke puncture.

will only take you a few minutes, so you can quickly be on your way. Fixing punctures is also great for people on a budget, as the price of a puncture repair kit is much cheaper than a new inner tube and will often repair a good number of tubes.

Difficulty – 2/5
Time – 20 minutes

Tools
Tyre lever
Puncture repair kit
Pump
Compressor (for tubeless tyres only)

Components
Inner tube (if required)

Step 1: Start by removing the wheel from the bike; most mountain bike wheels are designed to be removed easily and with the minimum of number of tools. There are several types of axle depending on the age and type of bike. Most are self-explanatory to remove, but if in doubt check the manufacturer's instructions. When working on the rear wheel select the highest gear and turn off the derailleur clutch if it has one. This should help relieve some of the chain tension and make the wheel much easier to remove.

Step 2: To remove the tyre you will first need to release all the air from the tube. For Presta valves you can simply unscrew the top of the valve and push the valve core in until there is no air left in the tube. For Schrader valves (car valve) you may need to use something thin like a 2mm Allen key or your fingernail to push the valve core in to release the air. To help remove the last bit of air from the tube, try to squeeze the tyre in conjunction with pressing the valve.

Step 3: Once the tyre is deflated, you need to unseat the tyre bead, which will make it much easier to remove. Starting at the valve, use both hands to pinch and pull the tyre away from the rim. As you go around the tyre you may hear it pop or ping as it becomes dislodged from the rim. Ensure the tyre is unseated on both sides before continuing.

Step 1: Remove the wheel.

Step 2: Remove all air from the tube.

Step 3: Unseat the tyre bead.

Step 4: Remove the tyre from the rim.

Step 5: Check the tyre.

Step 6: Find the puncture.

Step 7: Repair the puncture.

Step 4: Take a tyre lever and hook it under the tyre just to the left or right of the valve (normally its slackest point, which will give you more room to get the tyre lever in). If possible try to always use plastic tyre levers, as hard metal ones can cause damage to the rim and puncture the inner tube.

Once the tyre lever is in place, slide the lever away from the valve following the rim. If the tyre is not too tight you should be able to remove the tyre with just one lever. If the tyre is still too hard to remove with one lever, keep the first lever in and hook it over a spoke. Now take your other lever and slide it into the gap the first lever has made, using this second lever to slide the tyre off. Once you have removed one side of the tyre, you can push the inner tube valve into the rim and pull out the inner tube.

Step 5: Check the tyre. Once the tyre is removed you should now check for any sharp objects that may have pierced it and caused the puncture. First visually check the outside, the tread and the sidewalls, then check the inside by gently running your hand around the inside of the tyre. If you find any sharp objects such as thorns or nails pull them out with a pair of pliers.

This is also a good time to check tread wear and tyre corrosion.

Step 6: Find the puncture. First pump up the tube to see if you can locate the puncture hole from the sound of the air escaping out of it. If you have a small puncture or a slow puncture you may need to submerge the tube in water and look for the air bubbles escaping from the hole. Once you have found the puncture, mark the hole with yellow crayon so you don't lose it (usually supplied with puncture repair kit).

Step 7: Repair puncture. Start by roughening the area around the hole with some sandpaper. Then, if you're using glueless patches, you can stick the patch straight over the hole. However, if you're using glue, apply a thin layer to the patch and to the hole, then apply the patch to the hole and apply firm pressure for two to three minutes to allow the patch to bond.

Step 8: Reinstall the tube, tyre and wheel. Put a small amount of air into the tube, reinstall the valve into the rim and fully insert the tube into the tyre. Press the bead of the tyre back into the rim, starting with the tyre bead that is closest to the valve. Then slide your hands around the wheel rim ensuring the bead of the tyre pops back on to the rim. Pump the tyre up to the recommended pressure, usually displayed on the side of the tyre.

Puncture Prevention

To help prevent impact punctures you can use thicker, dual ply tyres, which will be harder to penetrate. Also using thicker inner tubes will help. DH-specific tubes are available for tougher applications and heavier riders.

To prevent pinch punctures try using a higher tyre pressure without exceeding the maximum usually written on the sidewall. Go up a couple of psi at a time until you find a grip/puncture resistance balance you are happy with.

To prevent spoke hole punctures, remove the rim tape and check there are no spoke threads that protrude above the nipple housing. If there are, they may require replacing for shorter spokes. Check the rim tape for damage and reinstall.

Step 8: Reinstall the tube tyre and wheel.

An example of a downhill tube.

Using a gauge on a track pump to ensure correct tyre pressure.

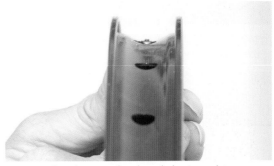

A spoke protruding through the rim eyelet.

Step 1: Remove tyre, tube and rim tape.

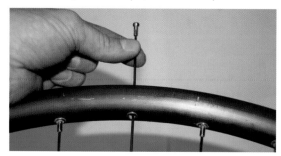

Step 2: Remove the broken spoke.

Step 3: Find a spoke of the correct size.

Step 4: Place the new spoke into the hole in the hub.   *Step 5: Get the correct number of crosses.*

Step 6: Drop the nipple on to the rim and thread onto the spoke.

How To: Replace Broken Spokes

Broken spokes are quite common and are caused by a number of factors including over-tightened spokes, using the wrong nipples, a broken or badly adjusted rear derailleur, or even just wear and tear. When you notice a broken spoke you should try to change it as soon as possible because it can dramatically reduce the strength of the wheel. If you start to break spokes more frequently this could be a sign of major rim damage, and the only solution is to replace the rim accompanied by a full set of new spokes.

Difficulty – 3/5
Time – 45 minutes

Tools
Spoke key
T25 Torx Key
Wheel truing stand
Cassette tool
Chain whip
Pump
Spoke ruler or measuring tape
Parts
New spoke

Step 1: Remove the tyre, tube, rim tape, and also anything obstructing the hub flange such as a cassette or disc. It is not always necessary to remove the cassette and disc, but it does make the job a lot easier.

Step 2: Find and remove the broken spoke(s) from the hub and remove the nipple from the rim eyelet.

Step 3: It is important to replace the new spoke with one of the correct size. To find the right measurement, remove one of the existing spokes from the same side as the broken one and measure it from the end of the thread to where it bends.

Step 4: Thread the new spoke (s) into the hub flange, making sure it sits into the correct side. Notice how the spokes are either placed into the hub from the outside of the hub or from the inside of the hub, remember to follow this pattern when replacing the new spoke.

Step 5: Take a look at the other spokes and notice how many times one crosses the other spokes before reaching the nipple; the most common is three times, known as 'three cross'. With a three-cross pattern a spoke will normally pass under two spokes and over one, or pass over two spokes and under one. Follow this pattern with the replacement spoke(s).

Step 6: Drop the nipple into the rim hole and thread the spoke into the nipple using a spoke key or a screwdriver to tension the spoke so it has an equal tension to the rest of the wheel. For deep rims push a matchstick on to the nipple or thread it on to the end an old spoke so that you do not lose the nipple inside the rim. Place the wheel in a truing stand and true the wheel (*see* Chapter 6: How To: True a Wheel). To prevent the nipple getting lost in the rim, push a matchstick into the top; this should help you guide it into the rim eyelet. Once finished truing the wheel, refit the rim tape, tube, tyre, disc and cassette.

Bearings

Over time mountain bike wheel bearings wear out and will need to be replaced. If the wheel feels rough when spun, or if there is any wobble from side-to-side, then the bearings will need to be adjusted or replaced.

Hub Cartridge Bearing Replacement

If you ride a lot, particularly in wet conditions, you will notice that your hub bearings will start to feel rough. If they are left long enough they will develop play, making the bike hard to handle. There are a couple of easy checks you can do to see if your bearings need changing; start by spinning the wheel and listening for any loud grinding sounds. You can also check for any play by holding the tyre and moving it from side-to-side in the frame or forks.

Which Bearings do I Need?

Most bearings will have a code stamped on the rubber bearing seal, which can be used to order the replacement. To reveal this code you will need to remove the outer hub spacers and check the bearing code on both sides of the hub. When changing your hub bearings it's always worth purchasing good quality replacements otherwise you will find yourself having to change them again before you know it. If there is no bearing code printed on the bearing seal you will need to check with your hub manufacturer's specification.

Difficulty – 4/5
Time – 45 minutes

Tools
Rubber-head hammer or mallet
Socket the same size as the bearing
Drift
Cone spanners (15mm, 17mm)
Cassette tool
Spanner to fit cassette tool
Chain whip
T25 Torx wrench

Step 1: Remove the disc and cassette if working on the back wheel.

Step 2: Remove the hub spacers.

Step 3a: Remove the inner axle.

Step 3b: Remove the bearing.

Step 4: Clean the hub.

Parts
New bearings
Grease

Step 1: Start by removing the wheel from the bike. Then remove the brake disc, and cassette if working on the rear wheel. (*See* Chapter 8, How To: Change a Cassette.)

Step 2: Most hubs have two spacers that fit on the outside of the cartridge bearings enabling the wheel to sit centrally in the drop out. You will need to remove both of these spacers, but bear in mind that the process for removing them depends on the brand of hub. Some can be simply pulled off, others have a small grub screw that needs to be loosened before they can be removed, and others have a thin circlip that needs to be dislodged. If you are unsure about how to remove these spacers check your hub manufacturer's guidelines.

Step 3a: If working on the rear wheel you will need to pull off the freehub, being careful not to lose the pulls and springs inside the hub. Now it is time to remove the old bearings. This procedure will vary depending on the brand of hub. Some will require the axle to be tapped out by placing the wheel on a soft hub support (or an old cardboard duct tape roll will normally do the job) and then tapping the axle out with a soft-faced mallet. Some axles can only be removed from one side so if you hit it and it does not move, try the other side.

Other hubs will have the axle floating on the inside of the hub. In this case you need to push the axle as far as it will go to one side. Then use a drift and a soft-faced mallet to slowly tap out the exposed bearing. Every few taps move the floating axle to the opposite side of the hub so that you tap it out evenly, reducing any damage to the hub.

Step 3b: Once you have removed the axle, there will often be a bearing left in the hub and also a bearing left on the axle. Place the wheel over a hub support and tap the bearing out with a drift. To remove the bearing from the axle, place the axle in a vice with the bearing on top and tap it out with a soft-faced mallet.

On rear wheels you will need to check the bearings in the freehub. The freehub bearings don't usually need to be changed as often as the main hub bearings. To check the freehub bearings look for any signs of corrosion around the bearing. Then put your finger in the centre of the bearings and move from side-to-side checking for any play. Finally, spin the bearing to check they are still running smooth.

Step 4: Once the old bearings are out, clean the inside of the hub with a degreaser; an alcohol-based disc brake cleaner usually works well. Then apply a thin layer of bearing grease to where the new bearings will be housed.

Step 5a: For best results when installing new bearings it is recommended that you use a bearing press. Carefully line up the new bearing up with the housing on the hub and gently tighten the press until the bearings are fully pressed into the housing.

Step 5b: If you do not have a bearing press, you will need to find a socket exactly the same size as the outer diameter of the bearing. Then place the wheel over a hub support, with the bearing lined up with the housing on the hub. Line a socket up with the bearing, while gently tapping the socket and applying pressure evenly to the bearing. If the bearing starts going in at an angle, it's best to tap it out, reseat it and try again. You should hear when the bearing is seated fully in the hub as the tone of the tapping will change. When one bearing is in, replace the axle and tap in the other bearing the same way as the first.

Step 6: Reinstall the outer hub spacers that sit over the bearings. If working on a rear wheel, make sure that all the freehub pulls are in position and then spin the freehub anticlockwise while pushing the freehub back into the hub. This will help the spring-loaded pulls sit back into the hub.

Finish by reinstalling any discs or cassettes and re-attach the wheel to the bike. Check to see if the wheel spins freely and that there is no play. If the freehub is locking up, check that you have not left out a spacer that sits between the freehub and the inner bearings.

Step 5a: Press the new bearings in with a bearing press.

Step 5b: Alternatively, tap in the new bearings with a socket.

Step 6: Reinstall the freehub body, spacers and cassette.

Step 1: Remove disc and cassette if applicable.

Step 2: Remove seals and loosen lock nut.

Step 3: Unscrew and remove lock nut and inner cone nut.

Cup and Cone Servicing

Cup and cone bearings have the advantage over sealed cartridge bearings in that they can be cleaned and serviced, making them last longer. Also, cup and cone bearings can be tightened up if you notice any excess play.

Difficulty – 3/5
Time – 45 minutes

Tools
Cone spanners

Step 1: Remove any quick release or bolt-through axles. Take off the brake disc if applicable, this will give you enough space to get the cone spanners into place. When working on the rear hub also remove the cassette.

Step 2: Most cup and cone hubs have a rubber seal over the outer cone nuts. This seal will need to be removed from both sides of the hub; normally this can pinch and be pulled off by hand. Once the outer seal is removed, place a cone spanner on the inner nut and another cone spanner on the outer lock nut. Holding the inner nut still, loosen the outer lock nut.

Step 3: Unscrew and remove the lock nut, then unscrew and remove the inner cone nut. There will often be spacers and seals between the lock nut and the inner cone nut, so make sure you lay them out in the order they were removed.

Step 4: Remove axle.

Step 5: Remove the remaining ball bearings.

Step 4: Position the hub over a large container to catch any loose bearings. Slowly remove the axle, while taking note of which side of the hub the axle is being removed from, as some axles are symmetrical. Fully remove the axle and place it on a paper towel or rag.

Step 5: Remove the remaining ball bearings from the hub shell, it may help to use a magnetized tool such as a screwdriver to help pick them up. Be very careful not to damage the bearing housing.

Step 6: Fully clean the ball bearings, hub inner and cones with degreaser; an alcohol-based brake cleaner normally works best, but most degreasers should do the job. Inspect the whole hub for damage or wear, paying careful attention to the bearings, cups and cones. The surfaces should be smooth and even. If the ball bearings are rough or dull in colour, they will need replacing. If the cones are pitted (dented), they should be replaced. The inner cups where the ball bearings sit cannot usually be taken from the hub, so if you notice any signs of damage or corrosion on the bearing cups then a new hub is needed.

Step 7: Now line the bearing cups with a thick layer of bearing grease. Carefully place the ball bearings into the cups, working on one side at a time. Once you have completed one side it may help to insert the axle and a cone to help prevent the bearings from falling out when the wheel is turned over to access the other side. With both sets of ball bearings in place, carefully push some grease in between the bearings and the cones.

Step 8: Screw on the cones, and reinstall any spacers or seals in the order they were removed. Then screw on the lock nut. Using the cone spanners, adjust the pressure on the bearings. If the cones aren't pressing on the bearings enough, there will be play in the axle. If the cones are pressing on the bearings too much there will be excessive friction and the wheel will not spin as freely as it should. Having the cones too tight will also wear the bearings out faster. It is a very fine adjustment to get the right pressure on the ball bearings. Remember that when the wheel is put on the bike and the quick release tightened, the cones

Step 6: Degrease and clean the hub and ball bearings.

Step 7: Apply grease to the bearing cups and reinstall the ball bearings.

Step 8: Reinstall the cone nut, spacers and lock nut in the correct order.

Step 9: Reinstall the disc and cassette if required.

get squeezed together. As such, you should leave a very small amount of play when the wheel is off the bike. Once you have found the right amount of tension, hold the inner cone in place with a cone spanner and tighten the outer lock nut against it.

Step 9: Refit any seals over the cones and then reattach the disc and cassette if applicable. Reinstall the wheel on the bike and tighten the quick release or

Step 1: Make sure the hub and rim are compatible, then find the correct length spokes.

Step 2a: Fit the first spoke.

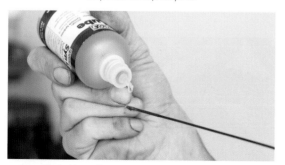

Step 2b: Apply spoke preparation compound to the spoke threads.

axle. Now the wheel should be running freely, without any side-to-side play. If you notice the wheel has play or if it feels too tight, you will need to remove it and readjust the cone tension.

How To: Build a Three-Cross Mountain Bike Wheel

You may need to rebuild a wheel because you crashed and damaged your rim or you might want to upgrade or build a custom wheel from new. No matter if you are building a front or rear wheel the process is similar. Hand-built wheels, if done correctly, can be stronger than factory-built wheels and will save you money, which can be used for other upgrades.

Note: When building a wheel there are many different spoke counts and lacing patterns to choose from. For mountain bikes we recommend using the most common three-cross pattern, but most of the techniques in this tutorial can be adopted for other spoke counts and lacing patterns.

Difficulty – 5/5
Time – 1 hour

Tools
Spoke key
Wheel truing stand
Spoke prep or chain lube
Spokes (correct length)
Spoke nipples

Step 1: Check the hub has the same number of spoke holes as the rim. Use a spoke calculator to find the correct length spokes for your hub and rim combination. If you are building a disc compatible wheel it will often require up to four different sizes of spoke.

For a rear wheel split the spokes into two piles, the drive and the non-drive side. For a front wheel just split into two equal piles of spokes. To find the length use a spoke online calculator:

- DTSwiss.com
- WheelPro.co.uk

- BikeSchool.com
- AppliedThought.com

Step 2: Apply a small amount of spoke preparation compound or chain lube to the threaded end of each spoke and a small amount to each hole in the rim to allow the nipples to be easily tightened.

If the hub has a logo, place a spoke into the hub flange from the inside to the outside of the hub on the drive side (non-disc side). If there is no logo just start anywhere.

Notice the holes on the rim are drilled off centre – this corresponds to each side of the hub (drive/non-drive). When a building rear wheels ensure you start with a drive side spoke, for a front wheel you can start either side. Insert this spoke into the hole left of the valve hole, making sure it corresponds to the correct offset rim hole. Screw a spoke nipple on just two turns. To avoid losing the nipple in the rim, you can guide it into the hole using a matchstick pushed into the nipple.

Step 3: Continue placing the spokes in the same pattern.

Step 3: Continue placing spokes into the drive side (non-disc side) of the hub flange from the inside to the outside, missing every other hole. Then insert a spoke into the rim and screw on a nipple (two turns) every fourth hole from the first spoke. There should be three empty rim holes between each spoke you place. When you place the spokes remember the offset rim holes should correspond to the drive side of the hub.

Step 4: Rotate the hub clockwise to allow space for the valve; this should follow the rotation direction of the disc if applicable. Fill the remaining holes on the

Step 4: Rotate the hub clockwise, and fill the remaining holes on the drive side.

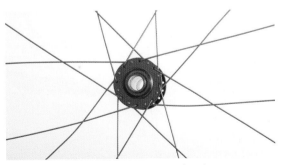

Step 5: Cross the spokes in an 'under, under, over' pattern. Continue until the drive side is completed.

Step 6: Thread the non-drive side spokesinto the largest gap created by the drive side spokes.

Step 7: Attach the first non-drive side spoke to the rim.

Step 8: Place a spoke to the left of the one you have just installed, then install a spoke into every fourth rim hole.

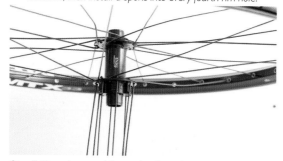

Step 9: Place the remaining spokes from the inside to the outside.

drive side with spokes from the outside in (opposite to the spokes you have already fitted).

Step 5: Now it's time to do the 'three cross'. Take one of the inside spokes and slide it diagonally under two of the outside spokes and then bend it over the top of the third spoke, so it crosses three spokes (hence the name 'three cross'). On the rim, fit the spokes to the middle of the three empty holes, continuing to match the corresponding offset rim holes. Continue this pattern until the drive side is fully laced up. It is a good idea to check your wheel against another wheel to make sure it is laced correctly.

Step 6: Turn the wheel to the non-drive side. Place non-drive side spokes from the outside of the hub to the inside, making sure the spokes go into the largest gap created by the drive side spokes. Make sure you place a spoke every other hole.

Step 7: Find the drive side spoke that's next to the valve hole and follow it back to the hub. Now find the spoke that's sitting directly opposite on the non-drive side. Take this spoke and attach it to the empty hole next to the valve hole on the rim.

Step 8: Place a spoke to the left of the one you have just attached and attach a spoke every fourth rim hole, starting from the spoke just attached next to the valve hole. Continue this pattern with the rest of the loose spokes.

Step 9: Place the remaining non-drive side spokes from the inside of the hub to the outside. Then take any spoke and make sure you pass diagonally over two spokes and then bend the spoke under the third

Step 10: Screw the nipples in, leaving about three threads showing on the spoke.

spoke. Now fit the spoke to the closest remaining hole. Continue this pattern for the remaining spokes. Once you have finished lacing the wheel check every spoke follows the three-cross pattern; it can be worth checking against another wheel to ensure you have not made any errors.

Step 10: Before you start to true the wheel, take a screwdriver and screw all the nipples in, leaving about three threads showing on the spokes.

How To: True a Wheel

Mountain bike wheels are kept straight, known as true, by spokes pulling against each other. Wheel truing is where you adjust the tension of the spokes to get the wheel running straight. You will need to true a wheel when building up a new wheel or when an old wheel becomes out of true from wear and tear. The principles of wheel truing are fairly straightforward but can take time to master, therefore it is recommended to practise on an old wheel first.

Difficulty – 4/5
Time – 45 minutes

Tools
Spoke key
Wheel truing stand

Step 1: Remove the tyre and inner tube from the wheel. Place the wheel in a truing stand with the right-hand side of the wheel in the right-hand side of the stand. If you don't have access to a truing stand you can turn the bike upside down and tie zip ties to the frame or forks in line with the rim (these can be used to help indicate where the wheel is out of true). Once the wheel is in the truing stand drop some lubricant on the end of the spoke threads – this will make the nipples easier to turn.

Step 2: (For a new wheel build only) Start with a spoke next to the valve hole and tighten every spoke in half-turn increments until the hub does not move from side-to-side.

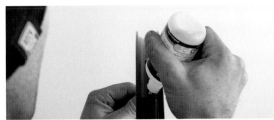
Step 1: Remove the tyre and tube, place the wheel in a bike stand and lube the spoke nipples.

Step 2: Tighten all spoke nipples until the wheel is tight (new build only).

Step 3: Check the dishing.

Step 4: Check the side-to-side movement.

Step 5: True the side-to-side movement.

Step 3: As the spokes gain tension you need to check the wheel aligns centrally in the frame or forks – this is known as 'dishing'. It is recommended to use a dishing tool for this task, although you can mount the wheel in the bike to see if the rim sits centrally. For more on checking and adjusting dishing please *see* Chapter 6: How To: Check and Adjust Wheel Dishing.

Step 6: Check and true the up and down movement.

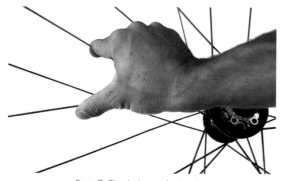

Step 7: Check the spoke tension.

Step 8: Relief stress on the spokes.

Step 4: Adjust the caliper on the wheel truing stand so that it is in level with the outer edges of the rim. Spin the wheel while adjusting the caliper until it scrapes lightly on the rim. This will indicate whether the rim is out of true laterally (side-to-side). If you find a rim misalignment, note where the caliper starts to scrape on the misalignment and note where it ends. You may find it helps to mark the rim misalignment area with chalk or non-permanent pen; this is the area that needs to be moved away from the caliper.

Step 5: Find the middle of the misalignment. Then tighten the nipple(s) by half a turn on the closest spoke(s) that pulls from the opposite side of the hub. For example: If the caliper touches the misalignment on the left side of the rim you will need to tighten the spokes that pull from the right-hand side of the hub. If you find the spoke(s) are too tight, you can loosen the spoke(s) on the same side as the misalignment, which is also often true when making any especially large adjustments. Once you have made an adjustment, spin the wheel and adjust the caliper closer to the rim to see if any further adjustments are needed. Remember, only make small adjustments otherwise you can create a lot more work for yourself. A wheel is usually considered true when there is no more than 1.0mm of side-to-side movement, although wheels that use disc brakes can be within 2.0mm.

Step 6: Now it is time to check for any up and down movement, also known as radial trueness. Adjust the caliper so it sits underneath on the rim. Spin the wheel and adjust the caliper so it scrapes on any low points of the rim. To make an adjustment, start by finding the middle of the lowest point and tighten the two closest adjacent spokes half a turn. If you notice any high points in the rim, find the middle of the misalignment and loosen the closest pair of adjacent spokes by half a turn. Repeat this process until the wheel is within 1.0mm of up and down movement. Remember, when adjusting radial trueness you should always adjust spokes in pairs; this helps to reduce the effect on the lateral trueness, although it is always worth checking the radial trueness every three adjustments of the lateral.

Step 7: Now is a good time to check the spoke

tension. If the spokes are not tight enough the wheel will flex and the nipples may loosen off, reducing its strength. If the spokes are too tight, there is a possibility of cracking the rim around the spoke holes. The best way to ensure you have the correct spoke tension is by using a tension meter. This is a relatively expensive tool for the home mechanic and is not essential. Spoke tension can be gauged by going around the wheel and squeezing two neighbouring spokes together, where there should be no more than a couple of millimetres of movement. For the more advanced mechanics it can be worth using a spoke tension gauge to experiment with different spoke tensions as it can dramatically affect how the bike grips in turns.

Step 8: Stress relief. It is important to relieve the stress on a newly built wheel to prevent it loosening off after a few rides as the spokes and nipples need to bed in. Place a piece of wood or something relatively soft on the ground. Put the side of the hub on the piece of wood. Hold the wheel on both sides and press gently against the ground; you may hear the spokes making a pinging sound. Spin the wheel around about 20 degrees and do the same again, continue this process all the way around the wheel, and then turn the wheel around and do the same on the other side. Now put the wheel back in the truing stand and check to see if the wheel is still true.

Note: After the first couple of rides it's worth putting the wheel back in the truing stand to check the spokes have not loosened off and the wheel is still in true.

How To: Check and Adjust Wheel Dishing

Wheel dishing is making sure the wheel sits centrally in the frame or forks. If the wheel is not dished correctly it can affect the handling of the bike and even cause the tyre to wear a hole in the frame. Dishing a wheel is made a lot easier by using a specialist tool that measures the dishing. If you do not have the tool you can normally mount the wheel in the bike and measure the distance between the rim and the frame or forks; although this method is not perfect it usually works sufficiently.

Step 1: Remove the tyre and tube.

Step 2: Place the dishing tool on the wheel and adjust the feeler gauge to touch the axle.

63

Step 3: Place the dishing tool onto the other side of the wheel, and check for gap.

Step 4: If necessary, adjust the dishing.

Step 5: Check the wheel is still true, and make adjustment if required.

Difficulty – 5/5
Time – 20 minutes

Tools
Spoke key
Dishing tool (recommended)
Spoke prep or chain lube

Step 1: Remove the wheel from the bike and remove the tyre and tube.

Step 2: Place the dishing took on one side of the wheel with the arms touching both sides of the rim, then slide the middle feeler gauge against the end of the outside of the hub. This is not the end of the axle, but the part of the hub that touches the inside of the frame or forks.

Step 3: Turn the wheel around and place the dishing tool on the other side of the wheel. If the wheel is dished centrally there should be no gap between the feeler gauge and the hub, and no gap between the arms of the tool and the rim. If you notice a gap, then the rim will need to be moved over to the opposite side of the gap.

Step 4: If you need to make an adjustment, start by adding a drop of lubricant to the top of each spoke nipple. If for example the rim is dished too far over to the drive side you will need to loosen off all the spokes half a turn on the drive side (right-hand side). Then tighten all the spokes on the non-drive side by half a turn. If the wheel is dished too far over to the non-drive side then you will need to loosen off all the spokes by half a turn on the non-drive side and then tighten all the spokes on the drive side by half a turn. Once you have adjusted both sides check with the dishing tool and make any necessary adjustments.

Step 5: Once you have finished dishing the wheel you will need to re-check the lateral and radial trueness of the wheel, if needed please *see* Chapter 6: How To: True a Wheel.

CHAPTER 7

CONTACT POINTS

This chapter looks at the components of the bike with which the rider comes into direct contact. Ensuring you have the contact points set up correctly for the type of riding you do will make your bike perform better, and give you a more comfortable ride. Even slight alterations to the contact points, e.g. changing bar width or stem length, can dramatically affect the handling of your bike.

Handlebars, Grips and Stem

The type of handlebar you choose should largely depend on the style of riding you do. The main factors to consider when buying handlebars are: width, rise, sweep, clamp size and material.

Width
The size of the handlebars you choose should vary depending on the discipline of mountain biking as well as the size of the rider.

Endurance disciplines such as cross-country use narrow handlebars, 620–720mm. They give the rider an aerodynamic, comfortable position for pedalling and for long periods in the saddle.

Disciplines such as downhill or freeriding usually use a wide handlebar, 730–800mm+. They increase stability, a big advantage when riding rough trails at speed.

Remember, it's always better to buy handlebars that are slightly too wide. You can experiment with width and cut them down when you have found the optimum size to suit your preference and style (*see* Chapter 7: How To: Cut Down … Handlebars).

Rise
The rise of the handlebar will determine where you stand over the front wheel. Flat or low-rise handlebars will help the front wheel grip in corners, and will also help the rider get his or her weight forward for steep climbs. Higher raised handlebars can give a more relaxed ride position and can also help less confident riders get their weight further

Different handlebar widths.

Aluminum handlebars.

Steel handlebars.

Carbon handlebars.

Different clamp sizes.

back over the rear wheel on steeper descents.

Bar Material

Handlebars are made from a wide range of materials, including aluminium, steel, scandium, carbon fibre, and even titanium.

Aluminium

Aluminium is the cheapest and most commonly used handlebar material. Aluminium handlebars come in different grades, typically between 2000 and 7000. The bigger the number, the higher the quality, and usually lighter the handlebar. High-grade aluminium needs less material to achieve the same strength as lower grade material.

Steel

Steel handlebars are great for dirt jumpers and freeriders who are not concerned about weight and want a strong and reliable handlebar. Steel has a higher tensile strength than aluminium. This means steel handlebars can be made using thinner tubing, giving the bar a bit more 'spring' and making it better at soaking up vibrations from the trail.

Scandium, Titanium and Carbon Fibre

If you are looking for the best lightweight handlebars then scandium, titanium and carbon fibre are the best materials money can buy. However, it's worth noting that the weight saving is rarely more than 100g and these materials can cost two or even three times the price of aluminium.

Clamp Size

The clamp size is the diameter of the handlebar where it is clamped by the stem. There are three main clamp sizes: 25.4mm is the more traditional size, the most common is the 31.8mm, called 'oversized', and more recently 35mm is becoming popular. The 31.8mm bar can be made to be as light as the 25.4mm bar but has greater strength and stiffness. The 31.8mm uses a thinner material than the 25.4mm, as the wider circumference leads to the improved structural strength and stiffness. Manufacturers are also now starting to produce 35mm clamp-size handlebars but these have not yet been widely adopted; many riders believe these handlebars may be too stiff and a certain degree of flex is preferable to dampen the bumps of a trail during long rides.

Bar Plugs

Bar plugs are vital for any mountain bike. Their purpose is to help prevent the open handlebar hole from filling with debris, and to help prevent injury. Remember to replace plastic bar plugs if they start to get a sharp edge, as they can cause injury.

Bar ends.

Grips

Although grips are a relatively cheap component they should not be overlooked as unimportant. The right grip should provide control in all weather conditions and also offer a certain amount of bump absorption. Grips come in a wide range of sizes, compounds, thicknesses, styles and fixing options. The right grip for you mainly depends on the size of your hand, riding type and a certain amount of personal preference.

Thicknesses and Width

Finding the correct thickness of grip for your hand size is important because if it is too thick it will make your hand tire quickly on long descents. If the grip is not thick enough it will not provide enough bump absorption, which will make the trail feel harsher than it needs to be.

The widths of the grips are especially important when it comes to riders with larger hands. If the grips are not wide enough their hands will be left protruding over the end of the bars, but if the grips are too wide it will limit access to the bike's controls.

Examples of thick and thin grips.

Fixations

Making sure your grips are secured correctly is important; the last thing you want is your grip to move when you're about to tackle a section of tricky trail. Over the years there have been a wide range of solutions to help grips stay in place – for example using glue and even wire. However, most modern bikes come with metal clamps that fasten the grip to the handlebar, these are called lock-on grips. Cheaper bikes will often come with slide on rubber grips that will work well in dry conditions, but may slide all over the place as soon as it gets wet.

Lock-on grips.

Examples of different grip patterns and compounds.

Compound and Pattern

The challenge of finding the right compound and pattern is not always easy and can be down to personal preference. The compound of the grip can act like suspension; the softer the compound the more bump absorption it will provide. The harder the compound the more feedback the rider will get from the trail, however it may give a harsher ride.

Conclusion

Due to grips being one of the cheaper components of a mountain bike yet also one of the most important, it's worth experimenting with a range of sizes and compounds. This will give you a better idea of your likes and dislikes, and can be a major help with providing a more comfortable ride.

Stem

The stem is the component that connects the forks to the handlebars. Changing the length of the stem will completely change how the bike handles. There are three main types of stem: a standard stem that clamps on to the outside of the fork steerer tube, a quill stem that bolts on to the inside of the fork steerer tube, and a direct mount stem that attaches to the top mount of a triple clamp suspension fork. The standard stem is most common, quill-type stems tend to be used on older or cheaper bikes, and direct mount stems are generally only found on freeride and downhill bikes.

Short stems (0–60mm) make the steering a lot more sensitive and will give you more leverage with the handlebars. Shorter stems are popular on downhill and freeride bikes where you need the

Long stem.

added benefit of increased control.

Longer stems (70mm+) are good to help keep your weight further forward on the bike to give a more efficient pedalling and aerodynamic position. This also helps to get grip on steep climbs and can make the steering feel less twitchy, which novice riders may find easier.

Pedals

Pedals fall into two categories: flat and clipless. The name clipless is historically derived from the rider's feet attaching to the pedals without the use of traditional straps and clips. Clipless does mean the rider's feet are attached, however. Cleats mounted on the rider's shoe engage with a mechanism and bind the foot to the pedal, allowing greater control and improved power transfer.

The alternative is 'flat' pedals; pedals without a clipping mechanism. Flat pedals are preferred by casual riders and riders wishing to take the feet off the pedals occasionally. Due to the improved power transfer and stability, racers of all disciplines prefer clipless pedals.

Quick Pedal Care Guide

Pedals usually have a hard life of getting bashed and battered off all sorts of things, but keeping them in good condition will help them perform better and last longer.

Check Pins

For flat, platform pedals always check all the pins are

Short stem.

Checking pedal pins are tight.

Checking for a bent pedal axle.

Threadlocking pins.

SPD cleats.

tight and replace any missing ones. This will help provide the maximum amount of grip, which could be the difference between a fun ride and nursing pedal scrapes on your shins.

Thread Lock Pins

The first thing you should do when you get new pedals is make sure all the pins are thread-locked in place; if you don't you will be surprised by how fast the pins will fall out.

Check Bent Axles

If you notice a strange wobbling sensation when pedalling, check the axle is not bent by spinning the pedal; if the pedal sticks in one area this may be the problem. To be sure, try another set of pedals and see if the problem persists. If it does it may be a bent crank arm that needs replacing.

Replace Cleats

SPD cleats are pieces of metal that attach to the bottom of specialist shoes. They connect the rider's shoes to a corresponding pedal. They are popular with endurance riders as they help improve pedalling efficiency. If you are using clipless pedals and you notice your feet unclipping easier than normal or you have more float than usual your cleats may need to be replaced. Compare your current cleats against a new set; if you notice the old ones are looking rounded and worn, try replacing them and see if it fixes the problem.

Grease Axle

It's important to keep your axle clean and greased so it stays running smooth and reduces wear. Some pedals have a grease port that will require either a grease gun or a syringe to fire grease into the axle, whereas other brands will require the pedal to be removed from the axle.

Anti-Seize

Use anti-seize on the pedal threads, which will help

Greasing a pedal axle.

Using anti-seize compound on the pedal thread.

Checking a clipless mechanism.

prevent the pedals sticking to the cranks.

Check Mechanism

When using clipless pedals make sure they are functioning correctly and are not damaged or missing any parts. Remember, the top and the bottom of the pedal should be the same. If needed, replace any parts and test in a safe environment.

How To: Install and Set Up a Bar and Stem

Changing the length of your stem and the width of your handlebars can dramatically change how your bike performs. Bar and stem installation is simple and is worth experimenting with, so you can see what feels right for you.

Difficulty – 2/5
Time – 15 minutes

Tools
Allen keys

Remove Bar and Stem
Step 1: Remove handlebars by completely unscrewing the mounting bolts and gently let the handlebars hang. Be careful not to damage any of the brake or gear cables.

Step 2: Fully unscrew the headset top cap bolt and then safely place to one side. Remove the top cap and any headset spacers that may be above the stem.

Step 3: Hold one hand under the crown of the forks, loosening off the stem bolts that clamp the stem on to the steerer tube and lift and twist the stem to remove. Make sure you continue to support the crown otherwise the forks could fall out of the headset, leaving you to pick up the pieces or potentially damaging the forks.

Step 4: There may be some spacers fitted underneath the stem; these can be used to adjust the height of the stem and handlebars. To adjust the height, either put spacers above or below the stem depending on what

Step 1: Remove the handlebars.

Step 2: Remove the headset top cap.

Step 3: Remove the stem.

Step 4: Place the spacers under or above the stem to adjust the handlebar height.

you want to achieve. Remember, there should always be at least a 4–5mm gap between the top of the steerer tube and the top of the stem or spacers above the stem (where the top cap pre-tensions the headset). Not enough space and you will not be able to tighten the headset, too much gap and your stem or steerer tube could fail.

Reinstall Bar and Stem

Step 1: Ensure your fork steerer tube and all the parts of the headset are correctly fitted in the frame.

Step 2: Slide the appropriate amount of spacers underneath the stem to achieve the desired stem height, then slide the stem on over the top. Ensure that the steerer tube is around 2.5mm from the top of the stem or top spacer, this space is to allow room

to preload the headset.

Step 3: Slot the bolt into the headset top cap and screw into the threaded star nut, this will tighten/preload the headset. Lightly tighten until the headset is tight, but the stem should still move freely in the headset. If you feel any tight spots, lightly loosen the top cap bolt.

Step 4: Fit the handlebars back into the stem, ensuring all the brake and gear cables are correctly routed. Then gently and evenly tighten all the bolts on the stem face plate. Tighten them half a turn at a time and in opposite corners to ensure the handlebars are square with the stem. Before you have fully clamped the stem on to the handlebars set the handlebar angle, roughly in line with the angle of the forks is a good starting point, then

CONTACT POINTS

Step 1: Check the headset is installed correctly.

Step 2: Double check the spacer height and fit stem.

Step 3: Preload the headset.

Step 4: Reinstall the handlebars.

Step 5: Align the handlebars.

Step 6: Check to see if the headset is tight.

tighten to the correct torque.

Step 5: Reinstall the front wheel and brake caliper. Now align the handlebars by holding the front wheel between your legs and twisting the bars until they are straight.

Step 6: Check to see if the headset is tight by rocking the bike back and forward with the front brake on, while using the other hand to take turns holding around the top and bottom headset cups feeling for any play. If you notice any play, tighten the top cap bolt more until it has gone. Once the handlebars turn freely without any play, tighten the stem bolts up to the correct torque.

How To: Fit a Star Nut

The star-fangled nut, or star nut, is used to pull the fork against the headset. This keeps the entire headset, fork and stem assembly tight. If you are fitting a new set of forks you will typically need to fit a new star nut after you have cut the steerer tube down to the correct height. Furthermore, over time star nuts can fatigue and slip inside the steerer tube, causing play in the headset and requiring the star nut to be replaced.

Difficulty – 2/5
Time – 5 minutes

Tools
Star nut setting tool
Hammer

Parts
Star nut
Rag/padding

Ideally remove the fork from the bike. If you are fitting the star nut to a new steerer tube make sure you have cut it down to the correct length.

If you need to remove an old star nut, knock it out of the bottom of the steerer tube with a long bolt or drift.

Step 1: Place some protective rag or padding over the fork dropouts and rest the forks against the ground.

Step 2: Screw the star nut on to the star nut setting tool with the flair pointing towards the handle. Remember, it's always worth using a new star nut.

Step 3: Line the tool and star nut so it's central over the top of the steerer tube. Use a hammer to tap the star nut into the steerer tube; this will take a reasonable amount of force. Keep on hitting the star nut setting tool until the tool is flush with the top of the steerer tube. If the star nut goes in slightly off centre, give the tool a few more taps with the hammer to line it back up.

Step 2: Screw the star nut on to the tool.

Step 3: Press the star nut into the steerer tube.

TOP TIP

If you do not have the correct tool you can use an appropriate size bolt together with an old top cap to help guide the star nut straight. However, it is always worth using the correct tool as one is relatively inexpensive and it will make the job a lot easier.

How To: Adjust Handlebar Width

Handlebar width is mostly down to personal preference. A good general guide is to have it around shoulder width. For XC and endurance riding, a narrower bar is generally preferred. For downhill and freeriding a wider bar is generally preferred. If you find your hands sitting right over the ends of your handlebars whilst riding or feel as if you are lacking a little control on technical trails then it may be worth trying a slightly wider handlebar.

If you are finding you are resting your hands on the inside of the grips whilst riding or think that your bike feels unwieldy on the trails then you may want to cut your handlebars down slightly. It is a good idea to slide your grips in on the bars to your desired width then go for a ride to make sure that the handlebar will feel good to you after being cut down.

Difficulty – 2/5
Time – 15 minutes

Tools
Allen keys or Torx keys
Tape measure
Hacksaw
Saw guide
Metal file

Start by removing the grips from your handlebars: this can be done with either a 2.5 or 3mm Allen key if you have lock-on grips, or by sliding and twisting the grip from the handlebars if you have regular grips. Loosen the bolts on the brake lever and gear shifter clamps and slide these off the ends of the handlebars.

Step 1: Most handlebars will have width markings stamped on the ends to aid cutting. Check and double-check these to make sure you are cutting to the right width.

Step 2: Take a hacksaw and slowly run the blade across the handlebar at your desired cutting mark. This will score the surface of the bar and make it easier to get a clean cut without the saw slipping.

Step 1: Double check where you would like to cut down your bars.

Step 2: Start the cut by gently scoring it with the hacksaw.

Step 3: Make a clean straight cut on both sides of the handlebars.

Step 4: Dull off any sharp edges with a file.

Step 3: Hold the handlebar steady, preferably in a soft-jawed vice, and use the hacksaw to cut through the handlebar at the desired mark. Try to ensure a clean straight cut. Repeat on the other side of the handlebar.

Step 4: Take a file and remove any burrs or sharp edges that have formed during cutting. Finish by reinstalling gear shifters, brake levers and grips. If you have a torque wrench, check all the bolts are torqued to the correct setting.

Saddles and Seatposts

The saddle usually supports more than half your weight while on the bike. Choosing the wrong saddle can put pressure on the wrong areas, causing a tremendous amount of discomfort, and even serious health issues. Furthermore, having the right saddle can be the difference between an enjoyable ride and an absolute nightmare.

Finding the right saddle isn't always straightforward; it can often be a process of trial and error. With a little knowledge, however, you can dramatically reduce the risk of purchasing the wrong saddle, and hopefully avoid getting a sore undercarriage.

When choosing a mountain bike saddle, the main factors to consider should be: gender, riding discipline and body shape.

Padding vs Weight

With saddles there is often a trade-off between soft padded types and hard ultra-lightweight race ones. This dilemma should only affect racers who are trying to shred every gram in order to have hopes for the podium. Recreational riders should take advantage of the extra comfortable padded saddles.

Saddle Holes

Most mountain bike saddles have a ridge or a hole in the middle of the saddle. This is not designed to save weight but rather to relieve pressure from the nether regions on longer rides.

Types of Saddle

General Mountain Bike Saddles

Standard mountain bike saddles come in many similar shapes and designs. They offer an average amount of support and cushioning while keeping the weight down. These saddles will often be adequate for the novice to intermediate rider who does not ride for more than a couple of hours at a time.

Women's Saddles

Most women's hipbones are wider than men, thus women require a wider saddle than men. Women's saddles usually have more padding to provide extra comfort.

Padded and lightweight saddles.

A saddle with a hole.

A woman's saddle.

A general mountain bike saddle.

A race saddle.

A gel saddle.

Race Saddle

Race saddles offer little in the way of padding. They are slim and lightweight, often being made from materials such as carbon fibre and titanium. This makes them pricier than the average saddle, but their slender design makes them more efficient for pedalling and less cumbersome on the descents.

Gel Saddles

Gel saddles are normally made from silicon-based gel that is designed to adapt to the rider's body, offering increased comfort. However, they can be slightly heavier than other saddles.

Types of Seatpost

When choosing a seatpost you need to consider the following factors: sizing, material and clamp type.

Sizing

There is a wide range of sizes when it comes to seatposts. It's important to make sure the diameter of your seatpost matches the internal diameter of your frame's seat tube. The two most common sizes are: 27.2mm (standard) and 31.8mm (oversized). Oversized seatposts have a larger diameter to help improve strength and are more common on modern mountain bike frames. If required you can use a shim to make a smaller seatpost fit a larger size seat tube. To check the seatpost diameter size either look at the existing post as it will most likely be stamped on there, or measure the inside of the seat tube with a pair of Vernier calipers.

Different seatpost sizes.

Materials

The two most commonly used materials are aluminium and carbon fibre. Aluminium posts are cheaper and inspire confidence when strength is needed, while carbon fibre posts are super lightweight and will give better vibration absorption.

Clamp Type

The majority of seatpost clamps are designed to be used with the standard twin rail saddle. Most clamping systems will allow you to adjust the position of the saddle back and forwards, and give the ability to adjust the saddle's angle either up or down. This is so the rider can set the position to his or her preference. Note that a small number of manufacturers use their own design such as a single beam clamp, I-beam or pivotal, which require a specific type of saddle.

A saddle clamp.

How To: Set Seatpost Height for Endurance Riding

Correctly adjusting the saddle position and height can dramatically improve pedalling efficiency and reduce the risk of fatigue, pain and injury. Before you get started make sure the suspension and handlebar position are set up correctly.

Standard Method

Step 1: Position the bike against a wall or ask a friend to hold the bike. Then sit on the saddle with your riding shoes on.

Step 2: Adjust the saddle height so your knee is not fully locked out when the pedal is at its lowest point. Your knee should have between 25–30 degrees of bend. Do this for both sides and find an average between both knees.

Step 1: Sit on the bike while the bike is supported.

Step 2: Adjust the saddle height so you have a sight bend in your knees.

Step 1: Measure the inside of your leg.

Step 2: Multiply the inside leg measurement by 109 per cent.

109 Per Cent Method

Step 1: Measure the distance from the floor through the inside of your leg to your crotch. Do this on both legs and take an average of them both.

Step 2: Multiply this number by 109 per cent. This is the number at which you should set your saddle height. Fully extend the pedal to its lowest point and then line the pedal/crank up with the seat tube angle. Measure from the pedal up to the top of the saddle.

TOP TIP
These methods are only a rough guide and if you experience any discomfort see your local cycle shop for further help.

How To: Set the Fore/Aft Position

The fore/aft saddle positioning.

Step 1: Sit on the bike with the pedals level.

The fore/aft position is the distance the saddle is away from the handlebars. It can be adjusted by loosening the saddle clamping bolts on the seatpost.

Step 1: Sit on the bike and put both cranks/pedals in the horizontal position.

Step 2: Adjust the fore/aft position so that the kneecap is directly above the pedal axle. This can be checked by using a piece of string with a weight on the end. If this cannot be achieved, you may need to change the size of your frame accordingly.

Saddle Tilt

The general rule for saddle tilt is to set the saddle flat, parallel to the ground.

Step 2: Adjust the fore/aft position so the knee is above the pedal axle.

Step 1: Measure twice, cut once.

Step 2: Clamp the saw guide in the desired position.

Step 3: Make the cut using a forward stroke of the hacksaw.

Step 4: Use a file to dull off the sharp, rough edges.

How To: Cut Aluminium Seatposts, Handlebars and Steerer Tubes

You may need to cut down components if they are too long or maybe even to save weight. Always double-check you are cutting in the right place, because after you have made the cut there is no going back.

Difficulty – 2/5
Time – 5 minutes

Tools
Allen keys
Hacksaw with a 32 TPI blade
Saw guide
Tape
Marker
File/sandpaper
Vice

Step 1: Measure where you want to cut and mark the area with a marker pen. If cutting down handlebars they normally have markers to help indicate where to cut. It is still worth marking the correct indicator with a pen.

Step 2: Clamp the saw guide into the vice. Slide the tube into the saw guide so the cutting groove lines up with your maker, then spin the tube to ensure it lines up all the way around. Once you are sure the saw guide is in the correct position, clamp the guide to the tube.

Step 3: Take the hacksaw and slowly start the cut. Remember that the saw blade is only designed to cut on the forward stroke, so releasing the pressure on the back stoke will prolong the life of the blade and save energy.

Step 4: Once you have cut right the way through, remove the saw guide and use a fine file to clean up any burrs or rough edges.

How To: Cut Down Carbon Fibre Seatposts, Handlebars and Steerer Tubes

Cutting down a carbon fibre seatpost, handlebar or steerer tube is a similar process to aluminium but has a few small differences. If done right it should require very little maintenance when finished, but if done wrong it could leave you having to replace the component. So take your time!

Difficulty – 2/5
Time – 10 minutes

Tools
Allen keys
Hacksaw with a 32 TPI blade
Saw guide
Tape
Marker
File/ sandpaper
Vice
Clear tape
Water

Step 1: Remember to measure twice, cut once.

Step 1: When cutting down anything, always 'measure twice, cut once' as a mistake at this stage could end up being costly. Remember, most frames require a minimum of 100mm seat tube insertion, so check with the manufacturer's specifications before cutting. If you are cutting down handlebars there are normally markers to help show where to make the cut. Once you are sure of where to cut, mark around the area with a marker pen.

Step 2: Wrap the cut marker in a single layer of electrician's tape. This will help prevent fraying while cutting and leave a clean cut.

Step 3: Clamp the saw guide into the vice and then insert the seatpost, bars or steerer tube into it so that it lines up with the cutting groove. Spin the tube to ensure it lines up all the way round with the cut maker (without rubbing the carbon on the guide). Once you are sure it lines up, clamp the saw guide to the tube.

Step 2: Wrap the cut area in electrician's tape to prevent the carbon from fraying.

Step 3: Carefully clamp the saw guide in the desired position.

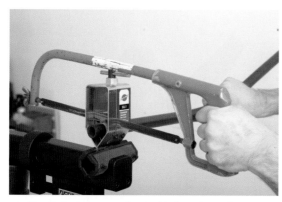

Step 4: Apply water to the saw blade and start the cut.

Step 5: If required, clean the area cut with fine sandpaper or a fine file.

Step 4: Apply a few drops of water to the hacksaw blade and slowly start the cut. Use the whole of the blade and only apply force when pushing forwards as the blade is not designed to cut on the back stroke.

Step 5: If you notice any small burrs or serrations, you can clean them up with a fine file or some sandpaper.

Dropper Seatposts

A dropper seatpost allows riders to adjust the height of the saddle whilst riding the bike, making it fun and safer on the downhill, and more efficient when

pedalling back up. Also, it helps to keep the flow of the trail without start-stopping all the time to adjust saddle height. The dropper seatpost has been a game changer for most mountain bikers, especially when it comes to race disciplines such as enduro.

Types of Dropper Post
When it comes to dropper seatposts there are a number of variables to consider.

Travel and Length
First think about the post length and travel. If you are tall and have a large frame then you will need a post that can offer adequate leg extension in the raised position, normally around 120mm in post-travel should be adequate, whereas riders with smaller frames may find longer posts a bit cumbersome.

Remote Lever vs Under Saddle Lever
There are normally two options when it comes to dropper posts: a remote lever adjusted from the handlebars or a lever under the saddle that requires the rider to remove a hand from the bars to adjust the saddle height. Most riders opt for the remote lever dropper seatpost because it is safer and quicker to adjust while on the move.

Cable vs Hydraulic
Remotely adjusted dropper posts either regulate the seat height by a mechanical cable or a hydraulic system. Mechanical systems usually require more maintenance than hydraulic systems, especially when riding in wet conditions. Hydraulic systems are often the better choice for a smooth lever feel and reliability.

How To: Bleed a RockShox Reverb Dropper Seatpost

The RockShox Reverb is one of the most common dropper posts out there and also one of the easiest to maintain and bleed.

Difficulty – 4/5
Time – 35 minutes

Step 1: Fully extend the reverb and carefully clamp in bike stand.

Tools
Reverb bleed kit
Torx keys
Rag or paper towel
Isopropyl alcohol/disc brake cleaner
Torque wrench
2.5 weight suspension fluid

Step 1: Put the dropper post in its fully extended position. Loosen off the seatpost clamp and raise the post to its minimum insertion point. Clamp the post in a bike stand, being careful not to clamp the hose. Rotate the bike on the stand so the remote is higher than the saddle.

Step 2: Turn the speed adjuster on the remote anticlockwise to its slowest position. Use a T-25 to loosen the remote and twist it around until the bleed screw reaches its highest point. Then retighten the remote in this position.

Step 2: Turn the speed adjuster to the slowest position and adjust the bleed screw to the highest position.

Step 4: Connect the full syringe to the remote and the empty syringe to the seat post.

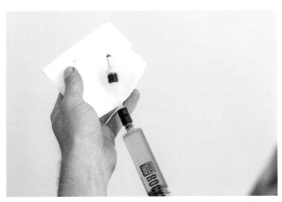

Step 3 Fill one of the syringes and remove any air bubbles.

Step 5: Push fluid from the remote syringe into the seat post syringe until you stop seeing air bubbles.

Step 6: Push firmly on the remote syringe, and then remove the seat post syringe, then reinstall the bleed screw.

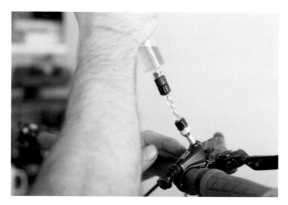

Step 7: Remove air from the remote.

Step 3: Fill one of the syringes with 2.5-weight suspension fluid (not brake fluid). Hold the syringe up right with a paper towel over the tip, then push then plunger to remove any air bubbles.

Step 4: Remove the bleed plug on the remote with a T-10 Torx key. Carefully screw the filled syringe into the remote. Remove the bleed plug from the post, located under the seat, and install the empty syringe.

Step 5: Hold both syringes upright, then push the fluid from the remote syringe while pulling against the seatpost syringe. Do this until there is no air coming out of the seatpost syringe, or there is about 10mm of fluid left in the remote syringe. If air bubbles continue, reverse the process until there are no air bubbles. It should not take more than a few goes. Finish with most of the fluid left in the remote syringe.

Step 6: Give a firm push from the remote syringe, then unscrew the syringe on the post and replace the bleed plug (the one with the O-ring).

Step 7: Pull up on the remote syringe while pushing the remote lever button in and out at the same time. Then push the syringe, which will extend the remote lever. Repeat this process until you see no more air bubbles.

Step 8: Finish the bleeding process by pushing the syringe in, then unscrewing the syringe. Replace the bleed plug with a T10 Torx key. If you have a torque wrench, tighten to 1.7n-m.

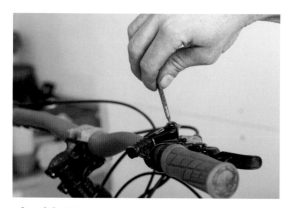

Step 8: Push the syringe in, before replacing the bleed screw.

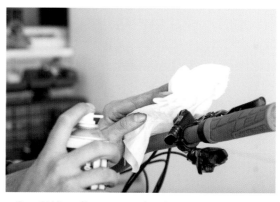

Step 9: Wipe off any excess oil, and reposition the remote.

Step 9: Replace the remote to the preferred position and retighten (5–6n-m). Wipe off any excess fluid from the remote and seatpost, then spray with isopropyl alcohol or disc brake cleaner. Remove bike the bike from the stand and reposition the seatpost to the preferred position.

Headsets

Although not strictly a contact point, the headset is a key part of controlling a bicycle's steering. The headset is the bearing assembly that joins the forks to the frame, allowing the bike's handlebars to turn.

A threaded headset.

Types of Headset

There are two main types of headset: threaded and threadless.

Threaded Headset

Threaded headsets work in conjunction with threaded steerer tubes. They can be recognized by the two flat nuts between the stem and the top headset cup. These flat nuts screw on to the steerer tube and are used to lock the headset tight. These headsets are rarely seen on modern mountain bikes and have been made almost obsolete by the threadless headset.

Threadless Headset

Threadless headsets are preloaded (tightened) from a bolt on the top cap that tightens against a star-fangled nut pressed into the steerer tube. This is then held secure by the stem pinch bolts that clamp on to the steerer tube.

An external headset.

The most common types of threadless headset are: external (standard), internal and integrated.

External

Also known as 'standard' headsets, they use bearing cups that are pressed into both ends on the headtube. The cups position the bearing outside the headtube, hence the name external.

Internal

Often known as semi-integrated headsets, they use cups that are pressed into the top and bottom of the headtube. These cups house the bearings inside the

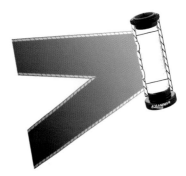

An internal headset.

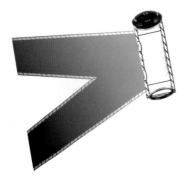

An integrated headset.

1in headtube.

frame, similar to an integrated headset.

Integrated

Integrated headsets are used on frames that have been made specifically so the bearings can fit directly into the frame. This makes them lighter because they do not require any cups. These headsets are commonly used on lightweight endurance mountain bikes.

Sizes of Headtube

When purchasing a new headset make sure it corresponds to the size of your frame's headtube and the size of your fork's steerer tube.

1in

These headtubes are ordinarily found on older bikes that are often used in conjunction with threaded steerer tubes.

1in

This is the standard headtube size for bicycles in general.

1.5in

These are used on downhill or freeride bikes to help improve strength.

Tapered

These headtubes measure 1.5in at the bottom and 1in at the top. They are designed to be used with a tapered steerer tube, although reducers are available to use 1in steerer tubes with tapered headtubes. The benefit of tapered headtubes is that they provide front-end strength while keeping weight to a minimum.

Offset Headset (Angle Set)

Offset headsets allow you to change the head angle (and subsequently the wheelbase and bottom bracket height) of your frame. This is accomplished by offsetting the two headsets holes into which the steerer tube fits. Offset headsets usually come in 0.5 degree increments which can be used to either slacken or steepen the frames head angle, depending on where the offset is positioned. A slacker head angle will give a little less grip for climbing and will make the steering slower, but will make the bike a lot more stable at speed, which is ideal for downhill and freeride bikes. A steeper head angle

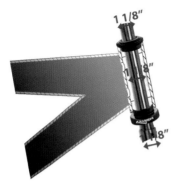

1–1in headtube.

Offset headset.

1.5in headtube.

Comparison of loose and sealed bearings.

Tapered headtube.

Step 1: Remove the front wheel and brake calliper, and loosen off stem pinch bolts.

Step 2: Remove the stem and tap steerer tube with soft mallet.

Step 3: Remove the headset cups with the headset removal tool.

Step 4: Clean and then apply a thin layer of grease to the steerer tube.

will make the bike climb better and more manoeuvrable at slow speed. There are many different types of offset headsets to suit different frame and steer tube combinations.

Bearings

There are two main types of headset bearing: loose bearings (non-sealed) and cartridge bearing (sealed). Both of these use preloaded ball bearings. The advantage of loose bearings is they can be easily serviced at home. The advantage of cartridge bearings is they are harder wearing and require less maintenance.

How To: Remove and Install a Threadless Headset

Over time headsets take a lot of punishment. This results in the cups wearing or becoming damaged, and eventually will mean the headset will need to be replaced. Installing a new headset is a reasonably simple job as long as you use the correct tools, otherwise you can risk damaging the headtube and requiring the frame to be replaced.

This tutorial focuses on fitting a standard threadless headset, but most of the principles will apply for other headsets.

Difficulty – 5/5
Time – 40 minutes

Tools
Headset remover
Headset press
Hammer
Mallet
Allen keys
Crown race setting tool
Crown race removal tool (optional)

Parts
Headset
Grease
Zip ties (optional)

Step 1: Place the bike in the bike stand. Remove the front wheel, front brake caliper and any guides or zip ties that attach the front brake hose to the fork. Loosen off the stem pinch bolts in sequence, but no more than a quarter-turn at a time. This will help decrease the risk of damaging any overloaded bolts. Remove the brake and gear hoses from the frame lugs close to the headtube. This will give you more space to move the handlebars and reduce the chance of kinking the hoses.

Step 2: Now remove the top cap, while holding your hand under the steerer tube to catch the forks in case they fall. Lift off the stem and handlebars and move them out of the way, being careful not to kink the cable. Take off any headset spacers and then tap the top of the steerer tube with a soft-faced mallet to separate the forks from the steerer tube. Place the forks safely to one side.

Step 3: Slide the headset removal tool into the headtube against the headset cups. It does not matter which cup you remove first, just make sure the edges of the tool are against the lip on the headset cup and not sitting on ridges in the headtube. Hold your hand over the cup you are about to remove and hit the tool with a hammer until the cup is almost out, tapping gently to remove the last bit. Repeat this process for both cups.

Step 4: Clean and degrease the inside of the headtube, then apply a thin layer of grease to help slide in the new headset cups. Place one of the cups on the headset press and slowly start to press the cup in (most headsets have a top and bottom cup, so make sure you install them correctly). Check the cup is going in straight, if not use the headset removal tool and start again. If fitting an external headset, make sure the logos line up between the top and bottom cups. Once you have pressed in both cups, inspect to see if they are sitting fully flush with the outer edge of the headtube.

Step 5: Now it is time to remove the crown race, this is the ring that is pressed on to the bottom of the steerer tube and helps preload the headset bearings. If you have the crown race removal tool, screw it firmly on to the crown race, then unscrew until the crown race slides free. You can remove the crown race with a flat-

Step 5: Remove and reinstall the crown race.

Step 6: Grease the headset bearing cups, and then connect the headset and secure by tightening the top cap bolt.

Step 7: Reinstall brake, wheel, etc.

89

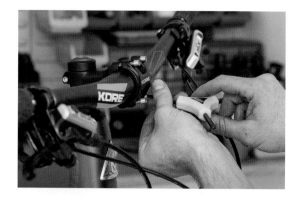

Step 8: Align handlebars and check for play in headset.

Step 6: Apply a fair amount of grease to the top and bottom cups; this is the same for loose or sealed cartridge bearings. Slide the fork into the steerer tube, making sure any seals are fitted correctly and don't get pinched. Add a thin layer of grease to the top of the bearing, then add the compression ring and headset top cover. Reinstall the headset spacers in the correct order to achieve optimum handlebar height and then slide on the stem. If fitting a new headset make sure you still have around 3mm between the steerer tube and the top of the stem, adding or removing spacers if required. Then reinstall the top cap.

Step 7: Refit the handlebars and front wheel, then re-attach the brake caliper with the brake hoses zip-tied or clamped correctly. Also, refasten the brake and gear hoses to the frame.

Step 8: Place the bike on the ground. Align the handlebars with the front wheel, tighten the bolt on top of the top cap above the stem until it starts to feel tight. With one hand, hold the front brake and with the other hand hold in turn each headset cup, while simultaneously rocking the bike backwards and forwards checking for any play or movement. If you notice any play, tighten the top cap bolt in small increments until it is gone. Then spin the handlebars from side-to-side to make sure there are no tight spots. If there are loosen the top cap bolt appropriately. Lastly, tighten the stem pinch bolts; if you have a torque wrench tighten to the manufacturer's recommended torque.

headed screwdriver and a hammer (although this not recommended as it can damage the fork). This is done by tapping each side of the crown race with the screwdriver, which will slowly edge it off. To install the new crown race, slide it down the steerer tube with the crown race setting tool and the matching adaptor. Hit the crown race setting tool with a hammer until you hear or feel a firm connection. Inspect to see if the crown race is sitting flush against the crown.

CHAPTER 8

DRIVETRAIN AND GEARS

The drivetrain, sometimes referred to as groupset, is the heart of the bicycle.

Without the cranks, chain, chainrings, cassette, derailleurs and shifters the rider would have no means to propel the bike forward.

In this section we will be looking at the assembly and maintenance of the bicycle's drivetrain and some of the problems you may encounter, plus the solutions to ensure all your gearshifts are smooth.

Chains

Modern mountain bike chains are variations of the roller chain. The roller chain was invented by Swiss engineer Hans Renold in 1880, although Leonardo da Vinci drew sketches of it 400 years earlier.

Chains are made up of links and each link consists of four parts: inner plates, outer plates, pins and rollers.

Which Chain do I Need?

Although most mountain bike chains may look similar, there are many different variants. Chain size is measured in pitch and width. MTB chains have a standardized pitch of half an inch, which is the distance measured between two adjacent rollers on the chain.

The width of the chain is determined by the amount of cogs on the cassette. This is because the width of the of the cassette stays constant, no matter how many gears.

So, for example, an eleven-speed chain will be significantly thinner than a nine-speed, as an eleven-speed cassette has to fit two more cogs in the same amount of space as a nine-speed cassette.

If you don't use a compatible chain it will cause shifting problems and will wear rapidly on both chain and cassette. So ensure you use the correct chain for the amount of gears you have on the cassette.

A standard chain.

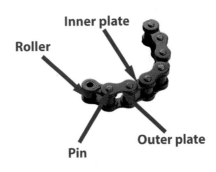

Showing the pitch and width of a chain.

When it comes to choosing a drivetrain manufacturer Shimano and Sram are the most popular, although other manufacturers do make compatible chains for both.

Common Chain Problems

Stretch

As a chain wears, the holes drilled in the inner and outer plates where the pins locate will become deformed and ovalized. This causes a tiny increase in the distance between pins, increasing the pitch and overall length of the chain. A stretched chain will not mesh correctly with the tooth spacing on your cassette or chainring, resulting in poor shifting performance, and cause the entire drivetrain to wear prematurely.

Wear

To check for wear you need to use a chain-stretch gauge, commonly known as a chain checker. This will quickly and accurately measure the distance between the chain pins and tell you if your chain needs replacing.

There are a number or different tools for this job: the Pedro's chain checker is ideal. If it hooks into the rollers of the chain, it means your chain needs replacing, simple.

Chain Suck

Chain suck is when the chain does not release from the bottom of the chainring and continues around, usually scraping the chain stay or bottom bracket and sometimes damaging the teeth on the chainring. The sudden stop in drive caused by chain suck can also cause the rider's knees to impact the handlebars or stem, causing injury.

The cause of chain suck is often a worn drivetrain. Usually the onset of drivetrain wear is due to a worn chain, which eventually wears the teeth on one side of the chainring and causes 'shark's teeth'. These hooked teeth don't release the chain as they should and result

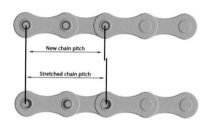

Showing chain stretch.

Showing chain wear.

Showing chain suck.

in chain suck.

Prevention is usually better than cure, as with most bike-related problems. If you do have chain suck, you should start by inspecting the teeth on your chainring for any signs of wear and replacing it if needed. Always replace your chain at the same time as your chainrings.

New bikes fitted with cheap components can have burred or badly made teeth on the chainrings. These can stop the chain from releasing correctly. If you come across any issues such as this, take a small half-round file and very lightly remove the burr or sharp edge.

Twisted Link

Twisted chain links can occur for a number of reasons: getting your chain jammed in a chain device or even during an awkward crash. Badly twisted links should always be replaced, but there is a quick fix solution.
Find the twisted link by spinning your cranks backwards and look down on the chain.

If there is only a slight twist, place an adjustable spanner on either side of the twisted link. Gently use the spanners to untwist the damaged link. If you're on the trail and need a quick fix, you can often untwist a

link by hand after fully removing the chain from the bicycle.

After a link has been twisted it should be replaced as soon as possible as it will have been dramatically weakened.

How To: Break and Install a Chain

You may need to split your chain for a number of reasons: shortening a new chain, repairing a damaged chain, or even replacing it when it's worn out. Using a chain tool to push one of the pins out of the chain is known as breaking the chain. Breaking chains should be kept to a minimum as each time you split a chain you weaken it slightly.

Difficulty – 2/5
Time – 5 minutes

Tools
Chain tool

Breaking the Chain

Before you break a chain with a chain tool, you should check to see if the chain has a power link (a link that allows the chain to be broken without the use of a tool). These links can often be found on Sram chains, although it's not uncommon to see split links on other brands of chain. *See* Chapter 8: How To: Split and Connect Powerlinks.

A twisted link.

Untwisting a twisted link.

Step 1: Secure the bike and drop the chain into the smallest cog on the cassette.

Step 2: Fit the chain tool to the chain and line the tool up with the pin on the chain.

Step 3: Start by pushing the pin out ¾ of the way out.

Step 4: Try to flex the chain apart.

Step 1: Secure the bike in a bike stand, or rest it on the ground upside down on the handlebars. Drop the chain in the smallest cog on the cassette; this will reduce the chain tension, making it easier to work on.

Step 2: Take the chain tool and slot the chain into the teeth furthest away from the handle. Screw in the handle of the tool, making sure the stud on the tool lines up with the pin on the chain.

Step 3: Before you start to push out the pin it's important to remember not to push it fully out, otherwise it will be extremely hard to get back in. Screw in the handle of the chain tool so it pushes the pin about three-quarters of the way out.

Step 4: Check to see if you have pushed the pin far out enough out by unscrewing the tool and removing it from the chain. Then flex the chain to try to unhook it from the last bit of pin left. If you have pushed the pin out enough the chain will pop off. If it's hard to remove, put the tool back on and push the pin out slightly further.

Reconnecting a Chain Without a Powerlink or Shimano Pin

Step 1: Reseat the chain back on to the pin you left protruding. To do this, squeeze the two ends of the chain together while flexing the chain away from the pin – you should feel it snap back together.

Step 2: Reconnect the chain tool, making sure the stud of the tool is lined up against the chain pin, and then screw the pin back in. Make sure there is an equal amount of pin sticking out both sides.

Stiff Link

After reconnecting a chain the link can become stiff, and if left will make your drivetrain skip.

To find a stiff link, cover your finger in a rag and place it under the chain while pedalling the cranks backwards. Normal links should roll over your finger with ease, whilst a stiff link will expose itself by not following the shape of the chain like the others.

Step 1: Flex and hook the chain onto the protruding pin.

Flexing stiff link with thumbs.

Step 2: Push the pin back through with the chain tool.

Once you have identified the stiff link, inspect the pin to see if it protrudes on either side. Attach the chain to the chain tool on the teeth closest to the handle; these teeth are used for removing stiff links. Screw the handle of the tool in so it lines up perfectly with the pin on the chain, Then keep on screwing until the pin is flush on both sides, trying not to turn more than a quarter-turn at a time.

If you're having problems removing the stiff link with the tool, or if you don't have a chain tool, you can place both thumbs over the stiff link and gently flex from side-to-side. You should slowly feel the link start to loosen. Don't flex too hard as you can easily twist the chain.

Shimano Chains

The pins on Shimano chains cannot be reused as they are made to fit perfectly into the plates of the chain. If you do try to attempt to reuse a Shimano pin they will normally be hard to press into the plate and will often cause damage. Instead, Shimano has its own pins and these help to maintain chain strength and shifting performance.

Buying Shimano Chain Pins

When buying spare Shimano chain pins you need to make sure you buy the correct pin that corresponds to the speed of your chain: nine-, ten- and eleven-

Finding a stiff link.

A Shimano chain pin.

Step 1: Join the two ends of the chain with a Shimano chain pin.

Step 2: Push the Shimano pin through with a chain tool until it clicks into place or the chain moves freely.

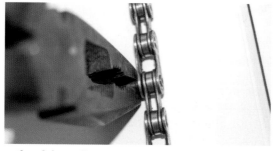

Step 3: Snap off the excess chain pin with a pair of pliers.

speed all requite a different pin. It's always worth buying a few extra to have as spare. A good tip is to keep a spare Shimano pin taped under your saddle for trail-side emergencies.

How To: Break a Shimano Chain

When splitting a Shimano chain you should avoid doing it at the factory-installed joining pin. This pin is usually clearly different from the other connecting pins, often being larger in diameter and a slightly darker colour.

Slot the chain on the chain tool's teeth furthest away from the handle, line up the stud of the tool against the pin of the chain and push the pin all the way out. For more information *see* Chapter 8: How To: Break and Install a Chain.

Rejoining Shimano Chains

Step 1: Line up the two ends of the chain and slot in the replacement pin with the rounded end first. The new pin should go most of the way through by hand.

Step 2: Unwind your chain tool right out to allow enough space for the pin, and slot the tool back on to the chain. Use the tool to push the replacement pin right the way through to the other side of the chain so it's flush with the outer plate of the chain. Remove the tool and check the chain moves freely; if not reattach the tool and press the pin in slightly further.

Step 3: Once the chain moves freely, take a pair of pliers and snap off the excess part of the replacement pin.

How To: Split and Connect Powerlinks

Powerlinks are special chain links mostly used with Sram chains that allow the chain to be split without a chain tool. Powerlinks can be very useful when you're out riding and you need to split your chain without a tool. However, ironically most new ten-, eleven- and twelve-speed chains are very stiff and normally require a special pair of pliers to allow the link to be removed.

Difficulty – 2/5
Time – 1 minute

Tools
Powerlink pliers

Step 1: Drop the chain in the smallest cog on the cassette, this will reduce the chain tension and make it easier to work on.

Step 2: Spin the chain backwards to find the Powerlink, it is usually a different colour to the rest of the chain. If you have a new Sram chain you will need to use Powerlink pliers because they are often too stiff to split with your hands alone. Slot the pliers between the two links and squeeze; you should feel the Powerlink click, and then pull apart.

Step 3: If you have an older chain you might be able to remove the Powerlink with only your hands. Place your thumbs on either side of the Powerlink and push together.

Reconnecting a Powerlink

Step 1: Hook a Powerlink on to both ends of the chain on opposite sides. Pull the chain together and slot the Powerlink into the corresponding holes.

Then pull both sides of the chain away from the Powerlink until they click together. On newer chains you may need to make sure the Powerlink is correctly seated by stamping your foot down on the pedals, which should make it click into place.

Chain Length

Fitting New Chains

It's important to note that if you are fitting a new chain it will usually need to be shortened. Also, when you purchase a new bike it's always good to check the chain length is correct, as it may have been overlooked during assembly.

A Powerlink.

Step 1: Drop the chain into smallest cog on the cassette.

Step 2: Find the Powerlink, and unhook it with Powerlink pliers.

Step 3: Older chains may be unhooked with just your hand.

Step 1: Reconnect the Powerlink and stamp down on pedals to ensure it is in place.

Getting the Derailleur Cage Length Right

It's important to determine if you have the correct length of derailleur cage. The wrong size derailleur cage will make it almost impossible to work out the correct chain length.

The size of the cage of the rear derailleur should match the ratio of gears.

For example: a cross-country bike with a wide range of gears will need a long-cage derailleur to be able to take up the extra chain tension through the whole range of gear combinations.

Whereas, if you have single chaining at the front and tight range of gears, as you would on a downhill hill bike, you can use a short-cage derailleur as there is less variation between the gears.

Chain growth (Full Suspension Only)

When setting the chain length on a full suspension bike you need to be aware of chain growth. Chain growth is when the distance between the rear axle and the bottom bracket gets bigger as the suspension compresses. You should always account for chain growth when checking chain length; failure to do so may result in damage to your drivetrain.

How To: Set the Correct Chain Length

Setting the right chain length is one of the most overlooked jobs on mountain bikes, and yet it's one of the most important. If you set the chain length too long it will be constantly be falling off and causing shifting problems. If the length is set too short it could cause your gears to jam and potentially damage the whole drivetrain, leaving you with a large repair bill.

Difficulty – 2/5
Time – 15 minutes

Tools

Chain tool
Power link pliers (Sram/KMC chains)
Need nose pliers (Shimano chains)
Zip tie (full suspension only)

Preparation

Bikes with front derailleur need to be shifted into the largest ring on the front.

For bikes with rear suspension it is necessary to compress or 'bottom out' the rear shock to set the minimum chain stay length.

For an air shock, let out all the air by compressing the valve core of the valve.

Step 1: Thread the chain around the largest front chain ring.

For coil shock you will need to remove the shock by removing the shock mounting bolts, then zip tie the frame into the bottomed out position.

Step 1: Take the chain and thread it around the front chainring, ensuring you pass through the front derailleur and any chain device roller or cage.

Step 2: Wrap the chain around the largest ring on the cassette and pull the two overlapping ends of chain together, without passing through the rear derailleur. Note the point where the chain could be joined at its shortest, remembering that only inner and outer plates can be joined, and then add two additional links to that length. This is your chain length.

Step 2: Thread the chain around the largest cog on the cassette, and pass it through derailleur wheels.

Step 3: Now rethread the chain back through the rear derailleur and check to see if the chain is long enough to fit around the biggest chainring and largest cog on the cassette with a little slack so the rear derailleur is not fully stretched. Then check to see if the derailleur has a little tension when in the smallest chainring and smallest cog on the cassette. If so, split the chain completely at this point.

When using a Powerlink, attach one half of it, pull together and note a position two additional links from the tightest point, remembering that split links join together from inner plates on both ends.

Step 4: Thread the chain through the rear derailleur and connect the chain. Finish by going through all the gears making the sure chain is not too tight on the larger cogs, or too loose on the smaller cogs.

Step 3: Pull the chain as tight as possible and join the chain two links back, giving two links of slack.

How To: Change a Rear Derailleur Cable

Over time changing gears can start to feel stiff, or they may not even shift at all. Replacing a gear cable is one of the simplest and cheapest ways to make your gears feel like new again. Sometimes you can replace just the inner gear cable if you flush the outer cable with some degreaser to make sure there is no debris trapped inside, although for best results it's recommended to change both the inner and outer cable at the same time.

Step 4: Go through the gears and check the chain is not too tight on the larger gears and not too slack on the smaller gears.

Step 1: Drop into the smallest gear on the cassette and loosen off the gear cable.

Difficulty – 2/5
Time – 15 minutes

Tools
5mm Allen key
Cable cutters
Pliers

Parts
Inner gear cable
Outer gear cable
Ferrules
Crimps

Step 1: Shift into the highest gear (the smallest cog of the cassette), unless you are using Shimano's less common rapid rise system, where you would need to shift into the largest cog on the cassette. Now loosen off the 5mm Allen key bolt that holds the inner gear cable secure.

Step 2: Cut off the cable crimp with a pair of cable cutters and pull the thick black outer cable away from the rear derailleur. This should fully remove the inner and outer cable from the derailleur.

Step 3: Remove the retaining cap or cover on the rear shifter. Depending on the make and model, this may require a cross head screwdriver.

Step 4: Pull the outer cable away from the shifter,

Step 2: Cut off the cable crimp and pull the inner gear cable away from outer.

Step 3: Some shifters have a rubber plug, which seals the gear cable, and this needs to be removed.

Step 4: Fully remove old inner gear cable.

revealing the inner cable. Hold and slide the inner cable into the shifter with one hand and, when the head of the cable appears through the shifter, pull it through until the inner cable is fully removed.

The outer gear cable can fill up with grime, which can dramatically affect shifting performance, so when possible change the outer cable at the same time as the inner. Remember, when buying outer gear cable it's always worth buying slightly more than you need because if it's too short you will have to go back to the shop to buy more.

Step 5: To ensure you have the correct length of outer gear cable, measure to size against the old cable. After you have cut your outer cable to length use a small 1.5mm Allen key to open up the hole on each end of the outer cable; this should help reduce friction and allow shifting. Now add a ferrule to each end and reinstall back on to the bike, leaving each end free.

Step 6: Take the new inner cable and line it up with the hole in the shifter from where you removed the old cable. Slide it right through until the cable head is seated well in the shifter.

Step 7: Insert the inner gear cable into the outer gear cable and push right through until you can pull it tight from the far end. Reinstall the ends of the outer cable into the shifter and rear derailleur. Pull the inner cable tight to help press the outer cable into position.

Step 8: Insert the inner cable into the rear derailleur, pull tight with one hand and tighten the 5mm Allen key bolt with the other.

Step 9: Once the inner cable is clamped securely, shift through a few gears and then drop back down to the highest gear again. This will help pre-tension the inner cable. Loosen the 5mm bolt again, pull the inner cable tight and retighten.

Step 10: Cut the excess inner cable off with cable cutters, leaving around 30mm of spare.

Place a crimp on the end of the cable and clamp it on to the cable with some pliers. Now is time to index your gears.

Step 5: Measure the new outer gear cable against the old one and trim it down to size. Then fit the new cable ends.

Step 6: Slide the new cable into the shifter, making sure the head of the cable is seated well in.

Step 7: Thread the new cable right through all the outer cable.

Step 8: Fix the inner cable to the derailleur.

Step 9: Shift up and down though the gears, then loosen off the cable from the derailleur, pull tight and reattach the cable to the derailleur.

Step 10: Trim excess cable and fit a cable crimp to stop fraying.

How To: Index Gears

With each gear shift the shifter should either release or retract the perfect amount of cable to move the derailleur smoothly across to the next cog of the cassette. Indexing gears is the simple of process of setting the cable tension correctly so that each gearshift corresponds to the matching gear on the cassette.

Symptoms that may be corrected by indexing gears: gear changes that are noisy or take time to change, the chain does not move up or down into the correct gear, or the chain moves up more than one gear at a time.

Difficulty – 2/5
Time – 5 minutes

Tools
5mm Allen key

Step 1: Release the cable tension on the rear derailleur by shifting the gears into the highest gear, the smallest cog of the cassette.

Step 2: Loosen off the 5mm Allen key bolt that clamps the gear cable to the derailleur. This will put the derailleur into its neutral position, which will be a good opportunity to check the limit screws are set correctly (*see* Chapter 8: How To: Adjust the Limit Screws on a Rear Derailleur), and also ensure there is no damage to the derailleur or derailleur hanger. If you have fitted a new derailleur or gear cable this step can be skipped.

Step 3: To index your gears you must first adjust the barrel adjusters located on the shifter and sometimes also on the derailleur. Turn the barrel adjuster fully clockwise as far as it will go, then one full-turn back anticlockwise. This step will help put the barrel adjuster in a good starting position. Reattach the inner gear cable, pull the cable tight with one hand and tighten the 5mm cable clamping bolt with the other. Be careful not to over-tighten this bolt or the cable may fray.

Step 4: Once reattached, pre-tension the cable by

pedalling the cranks forward, while shifting up and down through the entire gear range three or four times. Drop back into the smallest cog again. Loosen off the 5mm Allen key bolt, pull the cable tight and retighten the cable. This is to ensure there is no slack in the cable.

Step 5: Now check and adjust the indexing. Start by shifting up one gear. If it struggles to shift into the next gear, turn the barrel adjuster anticlockwise, in quarter-turn increments, until it shifts up smoothly into gear. Continue this process by shifting up through all the gears. One you have finished going to through the gears, shift back down through the gears. If it struggles to shift down, turn the barrel adjuster clockwise, in quarter-turn increments, until it shifts down smoothly. Once you have the rear derailleur shifting up and down smoothly your gears are indexed.

Step 1: Drop into smallest cog on cassette.

TOP TIP

Try a small amount of Teflon spray on the exposed inner cable and barrel adjusters to help keep the cable running smoothly.

Step 2: Loosen off the rear derailleur cable.

Step 4: Reattach the gear cable to the derailleur and go through the gears. Loosen off the gear cable, pull tight and again reattach the gear cable.

Step 3: Turn the barrel adjuster fully clockwise and then one turn anti-clockwise.

Step 5: Fine tuning the gears.

Step 1: Start by dropping into the smallest cog on the cassette.

Step 2: Remove the cable from the rear derailleur.

Step 3: Adjust the H screw until the top jockey wheel sits directly under the smallest cog on the cassette.

Troubleshooting

If your gears will still not shift up and down correctly, loosen off the 5mm Allen key bolt and hold the cable in your hand while shifting through the gears. You should feel inner cable move through the outer cable effortlessly as you click through the gears. If the cable feels rough or stiff to shift, try replacing the inner and outer gear cable and then re-index your gears.

How To: Adjust the Limit Screws on a Rear Derailleur

The job of the limit screws, also known as the end-stop screws, is to limit the movement of the chain in both the largest and smallest cogs on the cassette. Set correctly they should stop the chain from either jumping off the largest cog on the cassette and damaging the rear wheel, or jumping off the smallest cog and damaging the frame. Once the limit screws have been set up correctly they should rarely need adjusting, unless the derailleur becomes damaged or worn.

Difficulty – 3/5
Time – 15 minutes

Tools
Cross head screwdriver

Step 1: Change into the highest gear (smallest cog) while pedalling the cranks forward.

Step 2: Demount the cable from the rear derailleur by loosening off the 5mm Allen key bolt that clamps the cable. This is done so the cable tension does not affect the position of the limit screws.

Step 3: On the back of the derailleur you will see two screws close together labelled 'H' and 'L', which stands for High and Low. Start by adjusting the 'H' limit screw. Turn the screw clockwise, in quarter-turn increments, until the upper jockey wheel lines up directly under the smallest cog. Turn the screw clockwise to move the derailleur closer to the rear wheel and turn the screw anticlockwise to move the derailleur closer to the frame.

Step 4: When the 'H' limit screw is set, gently pedal the cranks forward and push the derailleur into a lowest gear (biggest cog), then release it. Once the derailleur is released it should quickly drop back into the highest gear. Repeat this process a few times to make sure the chain does not jump off the smallest cog on the cassette.

Step 5: Now to adjust the 'L' limit screw. While pedalling, gently push the derailleur towards the rear wheel into the lowest gear (the largest cog). Be careful not to push it too far and get the chain caught between the back of the cassette and the rear wheel. If the derailleur will not go into the largest cog you need to turn the 'L' limit screw anticlockwise until the top upper jockey wheel sits directly underneath the largest cog. If the derailleur starts to go off the back of the cassette, you need to turn the 'L' screw clockwise to limit the movement and keep the chain on the largest cog.

When you think you have got the 'L' screw set correctly, check it by pedalling and pushing the derailleur forcefully into the largest cog. If the chain runs smoothly and does not jump off the 'L' limit then the screw is set.

Step 4: While pedalling the cranks forward, push the derailleur into larger gears and let it drop back onto the smallest cog.

Step 5: Adjust the L screw so the jockey wheel sits directly under the largest cog on the cassette, and no further.

TOP TIP

Some mountain bikes have a plastic spoke guard that sits behind the cassette, known as a pie plate, this is to protect the spokes from the rear derailleur jumping off the largest cog on the cassette and damaging the spokes. If you have the 'L' screw set correctly it should not be needed and can remove it by taking off the cassette and unhooking it from the spokes.

Step 1: With the bike secure, remove the rear derailleur.

Step 2: Carefully screw on the derailleur hanger alignment tool.

Step 3: First check the vertical alignment.

How To: Align a Rear Derailleur Hanger

The derailleur hanger is a separate piece of metal that attaches the derailleur to the frame. The purpose of a hanger is to bend or break when hit hard enough to protect the frame and rear derailleur from damage. Hangers are usually made from a soft metal, making them prone to damage or misalignment. If the hanger is even slightly misaligned it can cause many problems with the gears: jumping, skipping or not staying in gear.

By straightening the hanger you can return your bike to peak shifting performance.

Difficulty – 3/5
Time – 10 minutes

Tools
Derailleur hanger alignment gauge

Components
Spare derailleur hanger (recommended in case of breakage)

Before you start it's important to make sure the rear wheel is true and correctly mounted to the frame, as this will be your reference point while using the derailleur hanger alignment gauge.

Step 1: Fit the bike securely into a repair stand and shift into the smallest cog on the cassette. This will leave you enough chain slack to remove the derailleur. Remove the derailleur from the hanger, then either cable tie the derailleur to the frame or let it hang out of the way, ensuring you do not damage any cables.

It's a good idea at this point to check the bolts that secure the derailleur hanger to the frame are tight, so the hanger does not move while being aligned.

Step 2: Install the derailleur hanger alignment tool by full screwing it clockwise into the hanger. Derailleur hanger threads are quite delicate so take time ensuring it is threading correctly.

Step 3: First check the vertical alignment by spinning the rear wheel so the valve is at the 6 o'clock position. Then adjust the feeler gauge on the tool so it is touching the rim next to the valve. Next, spin both the valve and the feeler gauge to the 12 o'clock position (this will be your reference point). If the feeler gauge is pressed firmly against the rim, or there is more than a few millimetres gap, you will need to make an adjustment.

Step 4: To make an adjustment, hold the top at the tool so you have the most leverage and push in the direction where the correction needs to be made. Remember to only make small adjustments and to always check each adjustment to ensure you have not bent it too far. Once straightened you need to check the horizontal alignment.

Step 5: Check the horizontal alignment by repeating steps 3 and 4, except use 3 o'clock as your starting point and 9 o'clock as your reference point. Once this is done, spin the feeler gauge all around the rim to make sure the gap between the gauges and the rim stay relatively consistent and make any adjustment where needed.

Step 6: When you're happy with the adjustments you can reinstall your rear derailleur. Once the derailleur is fitted you may need to readjust the limit screws and indexing as its position may have changed.

TOP TIP

If the derailleur hanger is very bent or showing signs of fatigue on the bend you will need to replace the hanger. If straightened it may fatigue the metal and could result in premature failure.

Step 4: Carefully make any necessary adjustments.

Step 5: Check horizontal alignment.

Step 6: Reinstall the rear derailleur and make any necessary adjustments.

Step 1: Remove the wheel from the bike.

Step 2: Use the chain whip and cassette tool to remove the cassette.

Step 3: Carefully reinstall the cassette with the cassette tool.

How To: Change a Cassette

You may need to change or remove your cassette for a number of reasons: the cassette could be worn out, you may want to change the gear ratio, or it may simply need a clean. When replacing the cassette make sure the speed of the cassette matches the speed of the derailleur and shifter. You can, for example, only pair a ten-speed cassette with a ten-speed shifter. Also remember when fitting a new cassette, it is recommended you fit a new chain at the same time, otherwise it may cause premature wear and shifting problems.

Difficulty – 2/5
Time – 15 minutes

Tools
Chain whip
Cassette tool

Parts
Cassette

Step 1: Remove the rear wheel from the bike.

Step 2: Remove cassette. Place the wheel on a flat surface with the cassette facing upwards. Take the chain whip and wrap it around the largest cog on the cassette in a clockwise motion. Then insert the cassette tool into the twelve-tooth locking nut positioned in the middle of the cassette. Turn the cassette tool anticlockwise while pulling on the chain whip; this will usually take some force and often makes a grinding sound when loosened. Once the locking nut has been fully removed, pull the cassette away from the freehub by pulling from the largest cog

TOP TIP

Whilst the cassette is removed it's a good idea to give it a really good clean with degreaser and a brush as it's tricky to clean whilst on the bike. Just remember the order of components!

at the back. If you are planning to refit the cassette, try to keep all the cogs together as it will make this easier.

Step 3: Some freehub bodies have twelve teeth, one of which is considerably smaller than the rest. Line this tooth up with the smallest groove on the cassette. Some Cassettes will just simply screw on, just remember not to force it and make sure the threads are lined up. Remember, when fitting a new cassette only replace it with the same gear ratio, otherwise it may not be compatible with the chain and derailleur cage length.

Step 4: Replace the cassette-locking nut, being careful not to cross-thread or over-tighten, as the threads are very fragile. Finish by reinstalling the wheel.

Step 4: Reinstall the cassette lock ring and fit the wheel back onto the bike.

Bottom Brackets

Most bottom brackets typically consist of a set of bearings with an axle through the middle, which allows the cranks to turn. There are two main types of bottom bracket: threaded, where the bottom bracket screws into the bottom bracket shell, and press fit, where the bottom bracket is pressed in like a headset.

Types of Bottom Bracket

Threaded
Threaded bottom brackets are either internal or external.

An internal bottom bracket.

Internal
Internal bottom brackets have bearings that sit inside the bottom bracket shell and ordinarily come with a fixed axle on to which the cranks are pressed. There are a number of different axle types, which must be matched to the cranks. The most common and least expensive is square tapered, but there are also a number of splined options available. These bottom brackets are normally used on cheaper mountain bikes, as the design is outdated, heavy and prone to wear.

External
On external bottom brackets the bearings are

An external bottom bracket.

A press-fit bottom bracket.

Bottom bracket spacers.

located on the outside of the bottom bracket shell. This means that the bearings can be larger and therefore harder wearing. The other advantage is the axle can be made of a larger tube with thinner walls, helping keep the weight down. The most common types of external bottom bracket are Shimano Hollowtech II, SRAM/Truvativ GXP and Race Face X-Type. The other benefit of external bottom brackets is they don't require any expensive specialist tools, making it easy for home fitting and servicing.

Press-Fit

There are two common variants of the press-fit bottom bracket, the PF30 and the BB30. In the PF30 the bearings are contained in a nylon or aluminium insert that is pressed into a threadless bottom bracket shell. The BB30 bearings sit directly into moulded bearing races on the inside bottom bracket shell. Both of these use a 30mm crank arm spindle, hence the name '30'. The big advantage with press-fit bottom brackets is they allow frame manufacturers to use thicker tubing; this helps to reduce weight and bottom bracket flex, thus increasing power transfer from the rider.

Sizes of Bottom Bracket

Threaded bottom bracket shells can vary in width from 68mm to 100mm or more. The two most common sizes of are 68mm and 73mm, although 83mm is a common standard for downhill and freeride bikes. The two most common press-fit sizes are also 68mm and 73mm, although they do vary in a range of sizes.

When buying a new bottom bracket ensure you have the correct size by measuring the current bracket and axle width with a pair of Vernier calipers. You can also check on the manufacturer's website.

Spacers

To achieve the correct chain line you will often need to use spacers on the bottom bracket cups. The amounts of spacers (if any) will depend on the width of your bottom bracket, the type of front derailleur and whether you have a chain guide. *See* bottom bracket manufacturer's instructions for exact configuration.

Chasing a bottom bracket.

Chasing and Facing

New frames can come out of the factory with deformities on the bottom bracket shell and headset. Chasing a bottom shell helps realign the thread and remove any burrs, making it easier to install a threaded bottom bracket.

Facing means to square off the outside of the bottom bracket shell; this helps centralize the bottom bracket, which helps to increase bearing life and reduces creaking. Most modern mountain bike frames should not need chasing and facing, but if your frame does need cleaning up it's worth asking your local bike shop as the tools are expensive and rarely used.

Facing a bottom bracket.

How To: Fit a Shimano External Bottom Bracket and Cranks

If your bottom bracket is starting to feel rough or developing play, then it's time for it to be replaced. Changing a bottom bracket may seem slightly overwhelming, but in fact it's very simple. The steps below are for a Shimano external bottom bracket, but these steps should be similar for most other brands, although the torque settings may vary.

Difficulty – 3/5
Time – 5 minutes

Tools
Allen keys
Bottom bracket tool
Crank install tool
Mallet
Flat-bladed screwdriver

Parts
External bottom bracket
Grease
Degreaser
Rag/paper towel

Step 1: Loosen off the Allen key pinch bolts on the non-drive side crank arm and remove the preload cap with the Shimano crank install tool. Unhook the plastic retaining clip located between the pinch bolts on the crank. Now remove the non-drive side crank

Step 1: Loosen the pinch bolts on the non-drive side crank arm.

Step 1: Remove the preload cap.

Step 1: Unhook the plastic retaining clip.

Step 3: Degrease the bottom bracket shell.

Step 1: Remove the bottom bracket spindle with a soft-faced mallet.

Step 3: Wipe away any grime or grease.

Step 2: Remove the bottom bracket cups.

arm by pulling it away from the bike. If the bike had a chain guide, remove both the top and bottom cages. Hit the bottom bracket spindle with a soft-faced mallet to release from the frame. You may need to pull from the drive side crank arm to help release it.

Step 2: Take the bottom bracket tool and remove the bottom bracket cups. Ensure the tool is well fitted to the grooves on the bottom bracket cups to prevent damage. To undo, turn the drive side cup clockwise and the non-drive side cup anticlockwise.

Step 3: Spray the bottom bracket shell with degreaser and clean out the old grease and threads with a rag or paper towel. Ensure threads are clean and check for any damage.

Step 4: Apply a thin layer of grease to the thread on the bottom bracket cups and the same to the threads on the frame's bottom bracket shell.

Step 5: Add the correct amount of spacers to the bottom bracket cups if needed; check the manufacturer's manual for more information on spacers for your set-up. Take the drive side cup (It should be marked on the cup either drive side or non-drive side) and gently screw the new bottom bracket cups in with your hands. If it feels tight ensure you are not cross-threading it. Remember to turn the drive side cup anticlockwise to tighten but on the non-drive side there is a regular thread, so turn clockwise to tighten. Use the bottom bracket tool to finish off tightening the bottom bracket cups flush against the frame. If you have a torque wrench, tighten to 34.5~49.1Nm.

Step 6: Apply a thin layer of grease to the spindle and push it in from the drive side, but be careful not to damage the plastic bearing covers on the outside of the cups. It's also worth hooking the chain over the spindle so it's easier to get over the chainrings; just make sure you don't get the chain trapped between the crank and bottom bracket shell.

Step 7: On the left-hand crank arm there will be a stopper plate positioned between the pinch bolts; its job is to prevent the crank arm from falling off if it comes loose. Take a flat-bladed screwdriver and unhook the stopper plate so it is sticking out. Then slide the crank arm on to the spindle; note that the crank arm will only go on one way, so don't force it. Once the crank arm is fully on the spindle, push down the stopper plate with a flat-bladed screwdriver so it helps hold the crank on.

Step 8: Reinstall the preload cap with the crank install tool. This cap is to preload the bottom bracket bearing and it does not need to be too tight. Once you have tightened the cap, spin the cranks to ensure they rotate freely and that the preload cap is not over-tightened.

Step 4: Apply a thin layer of grease to the bottom bracket shell and cups.

Step 5: Add spacers if required.

Step 6: Refit the spindle into the bottom bracket cups.

Step 7: Reinstall the plastic retaining clip.

Step 9: Push the stopper plate back between the crank pinch bolts with the side of a flat-bladed screwdriver. Tighten the pinch bolts and recheck they are tight. If you have a torque wrench, tighten to 9.9~14.9Nm. Hold both crank arms and pull from side-to-side to ensure the cranks are tight and there is no play. If using a chain guide, reinstall any cages or rollers.

How To: Install a Chain Guide

Chain guides are designed to stop the chain from coming off the front chainring(s) over the rough terrain, which is especially important for downhill and all-mountain bikes. There are three common mounting systems used to attach a chain device to a frame.

Bottom Bracket Mounted
Some older style guides are clamped between the drive side bottom bracket cup and the frame. Normally these are used on frames that do not have mounting tabs around the bottom bracket.

Step 8: Reinstall the preload cap.

ISCG (or ISCG Old)
This mounting system uses tabs connected to the frame around the bottom bracket. Some modern manufacturers do use this system but is usually only found on older bikes.

ISCG05
This system also uses tabs around the frame connected to the bottom bracket, but not in the same pattern as ISCG.

When purchasing a chain guide you may need to work out if your frame is using ISCG or ISCG05. To do this measure the shortest distance between the holes, ISCG will be 47.7mm and ISCG05 will be 55.9mm. Also check that the chain guide is compatible with the size of chainring you intend to use.

There are also adaptors available that allow you to use an ISCG or ISCG05 mounted chain guide that clamps directly to the bottom bracket.

The following tutorial should be similar for most chain guides, but always check the manufacturer's installation instructions before you start.

Step 9: Tighten the pinch bolts on the crank.

ISCG old

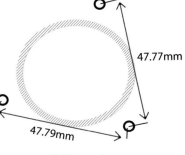

47.77mm

47.79mm

ISCG mounting.

ISCG 05

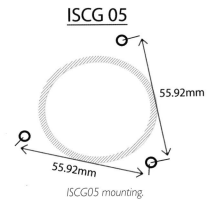

55.92mm

55.92mm

ISCG05 mounting.

Difficulty – 3/5
Time – 30 minutes

Tools
Allen keys
Bottom bracket tool (for bottom bracket-mounted only)
Crank install tool (Shimano only)
Crank extractor (if cranks are not self-extracting)
Mallet
Flat-bladed screwdriver (Shimano only)
Torque wrench (optional)

Parts
Chain guide (with corresponding mounting system)

Step 1: Place the bike in a bike stand and start by removing the cranks.

Step 2: Most chain guides will come with a selection of mounting bolts; short and long. If possible always use the longest set of bolts so you have solid connection with the mounting tabs. Approximate the amount of spacers you will need, if unsure start with one thin one and tighten the chain guide against the tabs. When using the longer bolts always check the protruding threads do not interfere or contact the frame when any rear suspension compresses.

Step 1: Secure the bike and remove the cranks.

Step 2: Mount the chain guide backing plate with spacers.

115

Step 3: Install the crank and chain ring. Then hook the chain over the chain ring.

Step 4: Refit the top cage and lower slider.

Step 5: Loosen the mounting bolts and position so the chain is central in the top cage.

Step 6: Put into middle gear on the cassette and check to see if the chain is aligned in the top slider.

Step 3: Check the chainring is mounted on the back of the crank arm mounting tabs. Remove the top cage and bottom sliders to allow enough space for the chainring when fitting the cranks. Reinstall the cranks; if you have a torque wrench check the manufacturer's specifications. Replace the chain back over the chainring.

Step 4: Refit the top cage and lower slider; some guides have markers depending on the size of chainring. Check the chainring lines up centrally between the top cage and lower slider. If the chainring does not line up you will need to add or remove spacers between the ISCG tabs and the chain guide. Remember never to space the top cage or bottom slider from the guide backing plate.

Step 5: Loosen off the ISCG mounting bolts and rotate the chain device so the chain sits in the middle of the top cage, not rubbing on the bottom roller. Also, make sure the bottom roller is not pressed against the chain stay, which can interfere with the suspension and damage the stay.

Step 6: Place the bike back into the bike stand and change gear so that the chain is in one of the middle cogs on the cassette. Now check to see if the chain is positioned centrally in the top slider; you should be able to see an equal amount of space either side. If the chain is not position in the middle you will need to add or remove spacers on the ISCG mounting tabs to correct this. Spin the cranks to check if there is any rub on the chain device. A small amount of rub can be common while the chain device is bedding in. Before riding give it a full bolt check and take the bike for a quick pedal around a car park to ensure everything is running well.

CHAPTER 9

BRAKES

The brakes are one of the most crucial components of a mountain bike. A good set of brakes allows the rider to feel confident in controlling their speed and lets him or her flow down the trail in a safe, but co-ordinated manner.

Correctly setting up and regularly maintaining your brakes will help ensure they work when you need them. Knowing you can trust your brakes will give you the confidence to ride the trail at your full ability, but it's worth bearing in mind that braking is a skill, and even the best brakes will not work correctly if misused. So remember, if going down a long descent try not to drag your brakes; with disc brakes this can cook the brake fluid, glaze the brake pads and scorch the disc, all of which will result in compromised performance.

Rim Brakes or Disc Brakes

In recent years bicycle brake technology has vastly improved. The majority of modern mountain bikes come with hydraulic disc brakes as standard, offering

Rim brake and disc brake comparison.

superior stopping power and greater reliability than the older style V-brakes.

The tried and tested V-brakes will, however, always be lighter, cheaper, and easier to maintain.

When choosing a new mountain bike or new set of brakes, you must first decide on the main use of the bicycle. If you're mainly riding rolling hills, canal paths and double track then V-brakes will probably suffice. V-brakes are also suitable for cross-country racers looking to save as much weight as possible.

If you are riding serious off-road, technical downhill sections, and in an area with long continuous descents then hydraulic disc brakes are the only real option.

Hydraulic disc brakes are also a better choice for riders who brave the winter months as V-brakes can suffer from mud gathering on the braking surface and greatly reducing stopping power. Disc brakes don't suffer this problem.

Mounting Points

It's important to note that V-brakes and disc brakes require different mounting points on the frame, forks and wheels. For V-brakes you need V-brake bosses on the frame and fork, and also wheel rims with a braking surface. If you're thinking about buying disc brakes you will need mounts on the hubs for the discs, and mounts on the frame and forks for the caliper.

V-Brakes

Cable-operated brakes such as V-brakes consist of four main parts; the lever, the cable, the arms and the pads. When the lever is pulled the cable is tensioned and the arms are drawn together by the cable tension. This forces the rubber brake pads to make contact with the wheel rim, and the friction causes the bicycle to slow down. V-brakes are relatively simple to set up and with some basic adjustments to accommodate pad wear and cable stretch, should provide many months of hassle-free service. However, over time V-brakes get worn and start to work less efficiently, especially if you regularly ride in wet or dry dusty conditions.

How To: Mount V-Brakes to a Bike

Many lower end or cross-country mountain bikes still use V-brakes. Learning to install and maintain them correctly will help to improve braking performance and also help ensure they are working when you need them the most. So if your brakes are feeling stiff or the cable is starting to fray, this tutorial should help you get your brakes running sharp and smooth again.

Difficulty – 2/5
Time – 15 minutes

Tools
Allen keys
Cross head screwdriver
Cable cutters
Loctite
Grease

Parts
V-brakes
Inner and outer brake cable
Ferrules
Crimp

Step 1: Remove the wheel corresponding wheel to the brake you are working on. Add a small amount of lock tight to the threads of the mounting bolt to stop them working loose. Apply a thin layer of grease to the outside of the frame or fork bosses, and then attach the V-brake arms using the single bolt on each arm. Some models of V-brake have a locating pin, which can sit in a choice of three holes on the frame boss. It's best to start with the pin in the middle hole and adjust later if necessary.

Step 2: Reinstall the wheel. Place the brake pads in the mounting points on the brake arms, making sure they are in the correct way around; the curve of the pad should follow the curve of the wheel. If the pad has a direction arrow printed on it, check it is pointing in towards the front of the bike. With the pad loosely placed in the arm, push the arm towards the rim until the pad sits flush with the rim. Adjust the pad position until the pad sits on the centre of the rim braking surface. If necessary you may need to move the spacers and conical washers around to get an optimum fit. Once the pads are in the correct position, tighten them while holding the pads in place to prevent them moving as they are tightened.

Step 3: Now adjust the spring tension by pressing the arm towards the rim and releasing, letting it return freely to its starting position. There should be a moderate amount of tension when pushing the arm towards the rim and it should return without assistance. If more tension is needed, turn the small adjustment screw until a suitable spring tension is achieved. At this point you may need to remove the arm from the frame boss and relocate the pin into a different hole on it to achieve the desired arm position and tension.

Step 4: Remove the grips from the handlebars and slide the brake lever on to the bar. Some levers can be fitted either inside or outside the gear shifter. It's best to experiment with both positions and find which position works best for you. On a mountain bike the lever should be positioned so it's operated by the index finger, or if you prefer both the index finger and the middle finger. This allows you to keep a good grip on the bar with your remaining two fingers and thumb. If the lever is positioned to be operated by all four fingers, the ability to maintain a good grip on the handlebars whilst braking is greatly reduced. Another advantage of positioning the brake lever inside the shifter is that the index finger is placed towards the end of the lever, giving more leverage and resulting in improved braking performance.

Step 5: Check you have the right brake cable; mountain bike brakes use a large cylindrical anchor,

Step 1: Lightly grease the brake bosses and slide on the brake arms.

Step 2: Reinstall the wheel and fit the brake pads.

Step 3: Set the spring tension.

Step 4: Position the brake levers.

whereas road bike cables use a thinner, pointier anchor. Fit the cable anchor into the slot on the end of the lever blade and then slide the rest of the cable through the lever. If needed, cut the outer brake cable down to size with some cable cutters. Measure by holding one end at the caliper and the other end at the lever, remembering the handlebars need to be able to turn 180 degrees. Check the ends of the outer cable for any burrs that may cause friction; if you find any cut them off with diagonal cutters. Fit a metal ferrule (an end cap) to the end of the outer brake cable and then thread the entire length of inner cable through the outer cable, ensuring that the adjustment barrel on the lever is screwed halfway in. By doing so, you leave room for adjustment later. Now attach the outer cable to the frame or forks.

Step 6: Thread the inner cable through the noodle, the small metal curved tube that sits in a groove on one of the brake arms. Loosely attach the cable to the other brake arm ensuring it sits in the groove and the bolt and retainer sits flush on top of the cable. Whilst

Step 5: Fit the inner brake cable to the lever and thread through the outer cable.

Step 6: Thread the inner cable through the metal noodle and fix to the brake arm.

Step 7: Fine-tune the cable tension with the barrel adjusters on the lever.

Step 8: Pull brake lever, checking both pads hit the rim at the same time.

holding the brake arms so the pads almost touch the rim, pull the cable tight and tighten the bolt that holds the cable in place. Cleanly trim the excess cable with some cable cutters, leaving around 50mm spare, and attach a crimp to the end of the cable to stop it fraying.

Step 7: Fine-tune the cable tension using the adjustment barrel on the lever. Either screw the barrel out to apply more tension to the cable, making the lever bite sooner, or unscrew to remove some cable tension to give more lever travel.

Step 8: Pull the brake lever and check to see if both brake pads touch the rim at the same time, if you notice one pad touching the rim before the other you will need to adjust the spring tension. There will be a small screw on the side of each brake arm; if you tighten the screw it will increase the tension, giving more pushing power to that arm. The aim is to adjust these screws so the pads hit the rim at the same time. Once adjusted check to see if the wheel spins freely and sits centrally between the pads. Finish by

inspecting to ensure the outer brake cable is securely in position and that the inner brake cable stays in place when the brake is pulled. Lastly, pull the brake lever hard eight to nine times; this will help bed in the cable and allow you to make any fine adjustments.

How To: Maintain V-brakes
As the brake pads wear down, the brakes will need to be adjusted to compensate. Usually this involves pulling more cable through so the pads are closer to the rim. If the pads have worn unevenly, they will need to be loosened off and adjusted so they sit flush on the braking surface.

One important thing to keep an eye on is the condition of the wheel rim. Over time, and especially with prolonged use on long descents and use in muddy conditions, the surface of the rim will wear down. When placing your finger on the rim it should feel smooth and flat. If the surface has a deep groove all the way around the rim, it is time to replace the rim.

Disc Brakes

Disc brakes can be either cable operated or hydraulic fluid operated. The main parts of the system are the lever, the cable or hose, the caliper, the pads, and the disc. Unlike V-brakes, which use the wheel rim as the braking surface, disc brakes have a metal brake disc that attaches to the hub of the wheel. The disc is usually attached to the hub with six bolts, however some Shimano systems use a centre lock disc attachment system. Adapters are available to run regular six-bolt disc rotors on a Shimano centre lock hub.

Disc Rotors
Brake rotors are available in different sizes; the bigger the discs, the greater the stopping power. A cross-

---

TOP TIP

Remember to use a small amount of lock tight on rotor bolts to stop them working loose.

Hydraulic disk brake. (By StromBer, via Wikimedia Commons)

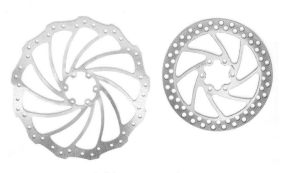

A disk rotor comparison.

Post mount

International standard (IS) mount

Types of disk brake mounts.

country bike would typically have lighter 160mm disc brake rotors, whereas a downhill bike would typically have 203mm disc brake rotors.

A great way to improve the stopping power of your brakes is to buy larger rotors. You will also need to buy a larger mounting adapter so the caliper sits at the correct position on the rotor.

Types of Disc Brake Mounts

There are two types of disc brake mounts available. International standard (IS) mounts have two mounting tabs 51mm apart, where the caliper is bolted to the mounting bracket. With this type of mount you will need to use an adapter to mount the caliper, and the front and rear adapters will be different due to the different distance from the hub to the centre of the mounting tabs.

The other type is 'post mount', where the caliper bolts directly to the frame or forks. If using a 160mm rotor you will not need to use a mounting adapter. To use a bigger disc rotor than this, you will often need to use an adapter. With post mount adapters it is important to take care not to damage the threads, as this will effectively write off the frame or forks.

How Often to Bleed Brakes?

If your disc brakes feel spongy, have excessive lever travel, or lack power they probably need bleeding to remove air from the system. Another indication that your brakes may need bleeding is if they have an inconsistent lever feel. It's good practice to replace the brake fluid every year and more often if you ride regularly.

Which Brake Fluid?

Some brakes such as Shimano use mineral oil, but many others use Dot fluid.

Dot fluid and mineral oil.

It's very important to use the correct brake fluid by checking the owner's manual or looking for some text on the brake system.

If you are using Dot fluid you should be aware that it is corrosive to paintwork and should be kept off skin by wearing gloves. If you do spill any Dot fluid on your paintwork its best to wipe it off as soon as possible. Dot fluid and mineral oil cannot be mixed or interchanged, so ensure you use the correct one. If your system uses Dot fluid you can use: Dot 3, Dot 4, or Dot 5.1. However, for a mountain bike never use Dot 5.

Tips for Preparing to Bleed Brakes

- It is extremely important to ensure that you don't contaminate your pads or rotor by getting brake fluid on them. Before attempting a brake bleed you should remove your wheel and the brake pads, placing them well away from your work area.

- Gently push the pistons back into the caliper using a tyre lever or something soft that will not damage the caliper pistons, remembering to apply even pressure to the piston. If you find one piston pushes in and the other pushes out, you will need to remove the bleed port screw or reservoir cap on the lever and push the pistons in. This will let out some fluid from the lever. If you do need to let some fluid out you may need to bleed the system after doing so if the lever feels spongy

- You should always fit a brake-bleeding block to the caliper. This is used to prevent overfilling of the system and will ensure the pistons are correctly spaced.

- Position the bike so the brake hose runs as close to vertical as possible from the lever at the top to the caliper positioned at the lowest point possible.

- Each brand of brakes has a slightly different bleeding procedure and this can also be model specific. In this book we have covered the most popular brands of brake, but remember to always check with the manufacturer's guidelines before you start the bleed.

How To: Bleed Shimano Brakes

Shimano brakes are one of the simplest brands to bleed and when bled correctly they usually require minimal maintenance. The main objective when bleeding brakes is to remove all the air from the system, so it's worth bearing in mind that air rises. You can help encourage this by tapping the brake hose.

One important thing to remember when bleeding Shimano brakes is that you should always use mineral oil, as dot fluid will damage the brake seals. There are many types of mineral oil but it's recommended to use Shimano-branded oil.

Difficulty – 2/5
Time – 15 minutes

Tools
Allen keys
Shimano bleed funnel
Syringe with tube
7mm socket or spanner
Brake block

Parts
Shimano mineral oil
Waste bag/container
Brake cleaner or isopropyl alcohol

Step 1: Loosen the lever clamping bolt and rotate the lever so the bleed port is horizontal. Remove the bleed port screw and screw in the funnel. If possible position the bike so the lever is higher than the caliper; this will help the air rise out of the system.

Step 2: Take off the wheel and remove the caliper from the frame or forks. Take out the brake pads, placing them out of the way where they will not get contaminated with oil. Push the pistons back with something soft like a plastic tyre lever, never use anything sharp because the pistons damage easily. Now insert a brake block into the caliper. The brake block is to ensure the pistons are spaced correctly and so that you do not overfill the system. Unclip the brake hose from the frame or forks to help the caliper to sit as low as possible.

Step 3: Fill a syringe with Shimano mineral oil so that it is two-thirds full. Remove any air bubbles by pressing the plunger of the syringe lightly with the rubber tubing pointing upwards and placed over a container to catch any excess fluid. Once you have removed all the air, attach the tubing to the bleed nipple of the caliper while keeping gentle pressure on the syringe to prevent any air getting in.

Step 4: Loosen the bleed port an eighth of a turn with a 7mm spanner. Gently push the brake fluid from the syringe at the caliper into the funnel at the top. If the fluid comes through dirty, fill the funnel so that it is two-thirds full, then install the funnel's thin plunger so the old fluid does not leak out and dispose of the dirty fluid. Re-attach the funnel and repeat the process until the fluid come through clean.

Step 5: Tighten the caliper bleed port and remove the syringe. Attach a section of tube to a bag, with other end connected to the caliper bleed port. With a 7mm spanner, quickly open and close the caliper bleed port while compressing the brake lever. Make sure to keep the fluid in the funnel topped up to prevent air being sucked back into the system. Repeat this three to four times or until there are no more air bubbles coming from the caliper. Once done, ensure the bleed port is tight and remove the tubing.

Step 1: Position the bleed port horizontally, and attach the funnel.

Step 2: Remove the brake caliper and pads, etc., then insert a bleed block.

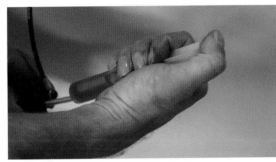

Step 3: Fill syringe two-thirds full with mineral oil and remove air from the syringe. Attach the tube to the nipple.

Step 4: Loosen the bleed port and attach the syringe. Push fluid from the syringe into the funnel.

Step 5: Attach tubing to bleed nipple on the caliper and gravity bleed into a container.

Step 6: Tap the brake hose and rapidly squeeze the brake lever to help any air bubbles rise into the funnel.

Step 7: Clean full brake system.

Step 8: Reinstall brake pads etc., and reinstall the wheel. Pull the lever rapidly in and out until you feel a firm bite.

Step 6: Squeeze the brake lever rapidly while tapping the brake hose to help pump out any air excess air. Once there are no more air bubbles appearing in the funnel, reposition the lever up and then down while pumping the lever. This will help make sure there are no air pockets in the lever. Make sure the oil level in the funnel does not get too low. When you see no more air bubbles in the funnel, plug the funnel with the oil stopper, remove the funnel and replace the bleed port screw.

Step 7: Remove the brake block. Use brake cleaner or isopropyl alcohol to clean the brake lever and caliper of excess oil.

Step 8: Reinstall the brake pads. Re-attach the brake hose and caliper to the frame or forks. Make sure the caliper is aligned correctly (*see* Chapter 9: How To: Align a Disc Brake Caliper). Pull the brake lever until you feel the pads are in firm contact with the disc. If the brake lever feels spongy or comes too close to the bar you may need to rebleed the brake.

How To: Bleed Avid, Sram and Formula Brakes

When your brakes start to lose consistency it might be because they have air in the system or that the fluid is old and full of debris, in which case you will need to bleed them. If you ride your bike a lot it could work out expensive to pay a bike shop every time your brakes need to be bled, so it's worth purchasing the bleed kit and oil and learning to do it yourself. The bleed procedure below will work for Avid, Sram, and Formula brakes, but it's worth noting that some models of brake may vary and that you should always check the manufacturer's guidelines. In this tutorial you will be using Dot fluid, which is corrosive so remember to wear gloves and wash any areas of skin that may come into contact with it. Also, Dot fluid can damage paint work, so after the brake bleed remember to full clean any appropriate areas of the bike with brake cleaner or isopropyl alcohol.

Difficulty – 2/5
Time – 15 minutes

Tools
Bleed kit (Avid, Sram and Formula)
Allen keys
Torx keys
Brake block

Parts
Dot 4 or Dot 5.1 brake fluid (depending on brake)
Rubber band
Brake cleaner or isopropyl alcohol
Gloves

Step 1: Half fill one syringe and quarter fill the other.

Step 1: Half fill one syringe and quarter fill a second (remember, it's worth using the brake manufacturer's own brake fluid because some brands can have additives that may not be compatible). Once you have drawn the fluid into the syringe hold the syringe upright and close the hose clamps on the hose. Pull on the plunger while tapping the syringe with the remaining hand to help any air bubbles rise to the top. Release the hose clamp and then push the plunger to push out any remaining air. It may help to hold a rag over the end to catch any excess fluid.

Step 2: At the caliper end remove the wheel and the caliper from the frame or forks. Now remove the brake pads, being careful not to contaminate them. Insert a brake block into the caliper to prevent overfilling the system and unclip the brake hose from the frame or forks to help position the caliper at the lowest point possible, which will help any trapped air rise.

Step 2: Remove the wheel, brake caliper and brake pads. Insert a bleed block to prevent over filling.

Step 3: Use a T10 Torx to remove the caliper bleed port screw. Attach the half-full syringe of brake fluid to the caliper while keeping light pressure on the syringe plunger to prevent any air getting in. Remember to be careful not to pinch the small black O-ring on the syringe bleed connector.

Step 4: If the lever has a contact point adjustment dial, turn it fully in the opposite direction to the arrow. Remove the bleed port screw on the lever with a T10 Torx and attach the quarter full syringe to the lever, again being careful not to pinch the black O-ring on the syringe bleed connector.

Step 3: Carefully attach the half full syringe to the caliper bleed port.

Step 4: Carefully attach the quarter full syringe to the bleed port on the lever.

Step 5: Push the plunger on the lower caliper syringe to force fluid and possible air into the syringe on the lever. It may help to pull gently on the lever syringe at the same time. Do this slowly until the caliper syringe is just under a quarter full. If you notice the fluid is dirty, push most of the fluid through to the top syringe and dispose of the dirty fluid. Continue to refill the syringes as in Step 1, and keep on pushing through to the top syringe until it comes through clean.

Step 6: To bleed the caliper, close the hose clamp on the lever syringe and gently push and pull on the caliper plunger to draw any air from the caliper. Keep doing this until you do not see any air bubbles rising from the caliper into the syringe. Finish the caliper bleed by applying pressure to the caliper syringe and closing the hose clamp on the syringe, then unscrew the caliper bleed connector and reinstall the bleed port screw.

Step 5: Push fluid from the caliper syringe into the lever syringe. If the fluid is dirty, repeat process until clean.

Step 7: To bleed the lever start by opening the hose clamp on the lever syringe. Push and pull on the plunger until you do not see any more air rising into the syringe. Now remove the lever from the handlebars and push and pull on the syringe plunger while holding the lever at different angles; this is to remove any air from any pockets in the lever.

Step 8: Once you stop seeing air bubbles rising into the syringe, give it one last push to fill the system and close the hose clamp. Then remove the syringe bleed

Step 6: Close the hose clamp on the lever. Gently push and pull on the caliper syringe to remove air from the caliper.

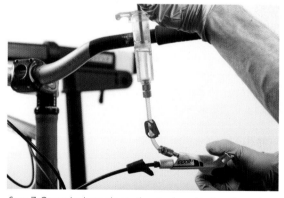

Step 7: Open the hose clamp, then push and pull on the syringe lever until you stop seeing air bubbles in the syringe.

Step 8: Remove the syringe and replace the bleed port screw.

Step 9: Clean the whole brake system with disc brake cleaner.

Step 10: Reinstall brake pads, caliper wheel, etc. Then keep on pulling the brake lever until you feel the brake bite the disc.

connector and replace the bleed port screw.

Step 9: Remove brake block. Then use a brake cleaner or isopropyl alcohol with a paper towel or rag to clean the brake lever, caliper and anything else on the bike that may have come into contact with Dot fluid.

Step 10: Reinstall the brake pads. Re-attach the brake hose and caliper to the frame or forks. Make sure the caliper is aligned correctly (*see* Chapter 9: How To: Align a Disc Brake Caliper). Pull the brake lever until you feel the pads are firmly in contact with the disc. If the brake lever feels spongy or comes too close to the bar you may need to rebleed the brake.

How To: Bleed Hope Brakes

Hope brakes are well known for being easy to bleed and maintain. There are a number of ways to bleed them, but it's always worth spending a bit more time to ensure you get a nice solid bleed, and ensuring you do not contaminate your brake pads or disc. When bleeding hope brakes you should be careful not to get any Dot fluid on your skin, and if you do you should wash it off as soon as possible.

Difficulty – 2/5
Time – 15 minutes

Tools
Allen keys
Torx keys
Hose
8mm socket or spanner
Bag/container
Brake block
Gloves (recommended)

Parts
Dot 5.1 brake fluid
Paper towel or rag
Brake cleaner or isopropyl alcohol

Step 1: Rotate the lever on the handlebar so the reservoir cap is horizontal. Use a Torx key to remove the reservoir cap and then carefully remove the

Step 1: Rotate the brake lever so the reservoir cap is horizontal. Remove the cap.

Step 4: Fill the master cylinder with Dot fluid.

Step 2: Detach the brake caliper, remove the brake pads and insert a bleed block.

Step 5: Loosen the caliper bleed nipple. Pull and release the brake lever until there are no more air bubbles coming from the caliper.

Step 3: Place one end of bleed hose onto the bleed nipple, and the other end of the hose into a container.

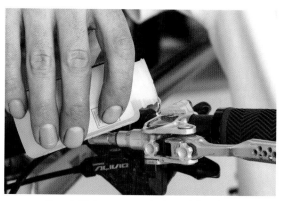

Step 6: Close the caliper bleed nipple. Quickly pull and release the brake lever until there are no more air bubbles in the master cylinder.

rubber diaphragm. Use a paper towel to carefully clean off any debris around the reservoir.

Step 2: Remove the caliper from the frame or forks and then remove the brake pads and place somewhere where they will not get contaminated with brake fluid. Insert a brake block into the caliper to help space the pistons correctly and ensure you do not overfill the system. Unclip the brake hose from the frame or forks to allow the caliper to sit as low as possible, which will help any trapped air rise out of the system.

Step 3: Push a length of clear hose on to the caliper's bleed nipple and place the other end of the hose into a bag or container. Place an 8mm spanner on the bleed nipple.

Step 4: Pour some Dot brake fluid into the master cylinder until it's full.

Step 5: Open the bleed nipple on the caliper a quarter-turn and slowly pull the brake lever to the handlebars and hold. Close the bleed nipple, and release the lever. When the lever is pulled the fluid and any air should flow out of the caliper. Repeat this process until no more air comes out. Ensure you keep the fluid level in the reservoir topped up otherwise you can end up sucking more air back into the system. If you notice the fluid is dirty, repeat this process until the fluid comes out the caliper clean.

Step 6: Make sure the caliper bleed nipple is closed tight and remove the rubber tubing. With the brake block still in, pump the brake lever in and out rapidly while tapping the brake hose. This will help remove any trapped pockets of air. Continue this step until you do not see any more air bubbles rising into the reservoir. By now the lever should be feeling firm when pulled, if not you may need to rebleed the system.

Step 7: Fill the master cylinder reservoir to the brim and replace the rubber diaphragm and cap.

Step 8: Remove the brake block. Clean the brake lever, caliper and any other components that came in

Step 7: Fill the master cylinder with Dot fluid, then reinstall the diaphragm and top cap.

Step 8: Clean the whole brake with disc brake cleaner.

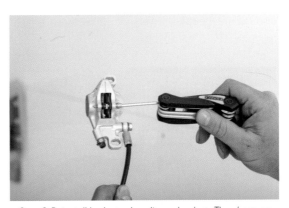

Step 9: Reinstall brake pads, caliper wheel, etc. Then keep on pulling brake lever until you feel the brake bite the disc.

contact with Dot fluid, it's recommended to use disc brake cleaner or isopropyl alcohol.

Step 9: Reinstall the brake pads. Re-attach the brake hose and caliper to the frame or forks. Make sure the caliper is aligned correctly (*see* Chapter 9: How To: Align a Disc Brake Caliper). Pull the brake lever until you feel the pads are firmly in contact with the disc. If the brake lever feels spongy or comes too close to the bar you may need to rebleed the brake.

Understanding the Brake Adjustment Dials

It's important to understand the purpose of the various adjustment dials available on hydraulic disc brake systems.

Reach Adjustment
The reach adjustment dial moves the lever closer to or further away from the handlebars. Riders with smaller hands or people who prefer to brake with one finger may prefer to have the lever sitting closer to the bars. People who brake with two or more fingers will need to have the lever further away from the bars so it does not hit their fingers while braking.

Free Stroke Adjustment
This is also commonly referred to as bite point adjustment or contact point adjustment. Turning this dial adjusts how much the lever moves before it pumps the fluid and the pads are in contact with the disc. Some people prefer the brakes to activate

Reach adjustment dials.

straight away while others prefer some lever movement.

How To: Shorten Hydraulic Brake Hoses

When buying a new set of hydraulic disc brakes they usually come with hoses that are too long; this is to accommodate different size frames and forks. Shortening the hydraulic hose may seem like a daunting task, but in fact it's simple and fairly quick. First of all, establish which is the front brake and which the rear. The front is the one with a shorter hose, but the rear hose normally needs more shortening.

Difficulty – 2/5
Time – 10–15 minutes

Tools
Set of spanners
Stanley knife
Vice
Plastic hose clamp
1.5mm Allen key
Torque wrench (optional)

Parts
Olive and hose insert (often the insert is connected to the olive).

Step 1: Place the bike in the bike stand, remove the wheel of the brake you're working on and squeeze the brake lever until the brake pads are almost touching. There is usually a rubber boot covering the hose fixing bolt at the lever, which you need to pull off. Unscrew the bolt fixing the hose to the lever with a spanner. Then firmly pull the brake hose out of the lever; it may help to move the hose from side-to-side to help the olive release from the brake. Sometimes this can be quite hard to pull out.

Step 2: Hold the hose up to the lever and mark the required length to be cut. There should be enough hose to allow the bars to turn 180 degrees to the left and 180 degrees to the right without the hose dragging or pulling tight. Also ensure you have enough

Step 1: Remove the wheel, and pull the brake lever until the pads are almost touching. Then remove brake hose fixing bolt, and pull the hose from the lever.

Step 2: Mark where the hose needs to be cut, allowing for handlebar and suspension movement.

Step 3: Make a clean cut and open the new hole with a 1.5mm Allen key.

Step 4: Slide the olive and fixing bolt over the hose. Clamp the hose in a vice with hose clamps. Tap the hose insert in with a hammer until flush.

hose for any suspension movement.

Step 3: Cut the hose using a sharp knife, being careful to get a clean cut. Then place the end of a 1.5mm Allen key in the hose to make sure the hole is open and has not been squashed. Make sure the end of the hose stays above the caliper to prevent the brake fluid flowing out.

Step 4: Clamp the hose using the plastic hose clamps in a vice, or you can use mole grips, making sure the rubber boot and hose fixing bolt is still on the hose. Slide a new olive on to the hose and press the hose insert into the end. Gently tap the hose insert with a hammer until it is flush with the hose. Bear in mind that with some brakes the hose insert and the olive are connected, but the procedure is the same.

Step 5: Place the hose back into the lever, and tighten the mounting bolt firmly to crush the olive so that it creates a seal.

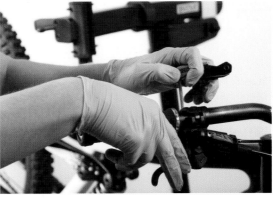

Step 6: Open the bleed port screw, then push the pistons apart, catching any excess fluid from the bleed port with a towel.

Organic (resin) brake pads.

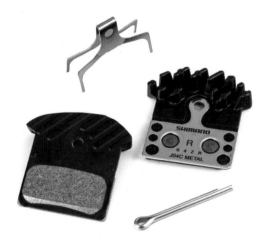

Sintered (metal) brake pads.

the pistons all the way in, but just enough so the disc will fit. Reinstall the wheel and keep pulling the lever until the lever feels like it is biting firmly against the disc. Reinstall the bleed port screw or reservoir cap. If the brake feels spongy or the lever travels to the bar, the system will need to be bleed.

Types of Brake Pad

Disc brake pads are available in a variety of compounds for different intended usage. There are two main types of disc brake pads:

Organic (Resin)
These are sometimes referred to as resin pads. They are derived from an organic formula and are a good choice for cross-country riders. They are very quiet in operation and offer a good lever feel. They wear down fastest in wet conditions but offer the best friction at slower speeds in dry weather.

Sintered (Metal)
This type of brake pad offers the best stopping power. They work well in muddy conditions and are long lasting, which is ideal for downhill use. However, they may give the brake a grabby feel and can often make a noise, especially in wet conditions. Brake pads can be found at a variety of prices, with the brake manufacturers' own brand usually being the most expensive (approx. £20). It's best to avoid the really cheap pads, as they are not likely to last very long and offer a decreased braking feel and power. A middle price range pad (approx. £15) will offer good value for money and nearly the same performance as the brake manufacturer's ones.

Step 5: Push the brake hose back into the lever, and tighten the hose nut. You need to apply enough force to crush the olive, 5–7Nm tightening torque. Once tight, cover the nut with the rubber boot.

Step 6: Position the lever so the bleed port of the reservoir is horizontal. Remove the bleed port screw or reservoir cap on the lever. Hold a paper towel around the lever to catch any excess fluid. Push the brake pads apart with a plastic tyre lever. Do not push

How To: Fit Hydraulic Brake Pads

It's important to keep an eye on your brake pad wear, because when they start to get low it can dramatically affect the feel and performance of your brakes. How you change your brake pads will often differ from brand to brand but the process is quite similar. Most brakes have springs that keeps the pads in position and some have a retaining pin that stops the pads from falling out.

When do Brake Pads Need to be Changed?

Even when mountain bike brake pads are new they only have 2–3mm of braking material, so it can be hard to know when to change them. It's recommended to change the pads once the braking material is getting close to the spring or about 1mm from the backing plate.

Difficulty – 2/5
Time – 15 minutes

Tools
Allen keys or Torx key

Parts
Isopropyl alcohol
Brake pads

Step 1: Unscrew the two caliper fixing bolts that fix the caliper to the frame or forks. If there are any spacers between the brake mount and the caliper, take note of which order they came out. It's often a good ideas to lay the spacers out in order to avoid any confusion.

Step 2: Remove the brake pads' retaining pin. Some pins have a small circlip to hold the pin safely in place; this will need to be removed first and placed carefully to one side. Some brakes use a split pin, which requires the use of a pair of pliers to bend it straight before it can be removed.

Step 3: Pull the pads out from the caliper. Some pads remove from the top of the caliper and others from the bottom. If they have a spring, squeeze both pads together and remove them all at once. Check to see if your new brake pads come with a spring and if not keep this to one side. If you find the pads hard to remove, push the pads back in to the caliper with something like a flat-headed screwdriver to create more space and then try again.

Step 4: Using a tyre lever or screwdriver, gently push the pistons back into the caliper. Make sure you apply

Step 1: Remove the caliper mounting bolts.

Step 2: Remove the brake pad retaining pin.

Step 3: Remove the brake pads.

Step 4: Push the pistons back with a plastic tyre lever.

Step 5: Clean the caliper and inspect it for damage.

Step 6: Fit the brake pad spring between the new pads and then fit the pads into the caliper.

Step 7: Reinstall the brake pad retaining pin.

Step 8: Loosely remount the caliper to the bike and tighten once centred over the disc.

an even pressure to all sides of the piston; push on both sides until the pistons are flush with the caliper body. If you push in one piston and the other pushes out, you will need to remove the bleed port screw on the lever and then push the pistons back while holding a rag over the bleed port to catch any excess fluid. Once the pistons are back, reinstall the bleed port screw.

Step 5: Clean the caliper with brake cleaner or isopropyl alcohol and wipe with a paper towel or rag. Now is a good opportunity to inspect the pistons for damage or leakages.

Step 6: Fit the pad spring between the pads and squeeze the pads together, then slide the new pads into the caliper.

Step 7: Replace the retaining pin and circlip, or if using a split pin slide it through the caliper and bend the end over to stop it from falling out.

Step 8: Remount the caliper loosely to the bike with the two fixing bolts. Make sure you reinstall any spacers in the correct order, although some brakes do not use spacers. Before tightening the caliper look down at the brake pads and disc, try to line them up so you can see an equal amount of space between the pads and disc on both sides, and then tighten.

Step 9: Squeeze the brake lever until the pads are in contact with the disc rotor. Spin the wheel and if the disc is rubbing, realign the caliper. (*See below*: How To: Align a Disc Brake Caliper). Finish by bedding the new pads in by riding on flat ground and braking hard. Repeat this process fifteen to twenty times.

Step 9: Pull the brake lever until the caliper firmly bites the disc. Spin the wheel and realign the caliper if you notice any rubbing.

How To: Align a Disc Brake Caliper to Stop it Rubbing

After changing brake pads, fitting new brakes, or reattaching a caliper it is important to get the caliper lined up with the disc so the pads aren't rubbing. By aligning the caliper you can stop the annoying rubbing sound and also improve braking performance.

Difficulty – 1/5
Time – 5 minutes

Tools
Allen keys

Step 1: Loosen the two caliper bolts enough so you can move the caliper without it jumping out of place.

Step 2: Look at the caliper from where the disc passes through it. Check to see if the pistons are pushing an equal amount from both sides. It's important for braking performance to have both pistons pushing an equal amount. If you notice one piston sticking out more than the other you will need to fully remove the caliper and push both pistons fully back into the caliper body with a plastic tyre lever. Then reinstall the caliper.

Step 3: Look at the caliper from where the disc passes through between the brake pads. Carefully line up the caliper so you can see an equal amount of space between the brake pads and the disc on both sides. Once the disc is lined up, secure the caliper mounting bolts in place.

Step 4: Pump the brake lever until you feel the brake bite. Then spin the wheel to check the pads don't rub on the disc, and visually check that the disc runs through the middle of the caliper without catching. If you notice the disc is catching in one area the disc might be bent.

How To: Straighten a Bent Disc Rotor

When aligning the caliper, if the disc is still catching it

Step 1: Loosen the caliper mounting bolts.

Step 2: Check that the pistons are protruding equally. If not, reset them by pushing them back into the caliper with a plastic tyre lever.

Step 3: It can be hard to see, but try to line the disc up so that it sits centrally between the brake pads, then secure the mounting bolts.

Step 4: Spin the wheel to check for rubbing. If it rubs repeat steps 2 and 3. If that does not solve the problem, the disc might be bent.

Step 1: Spin the wheel to locate the bend.

Step 2: Take a marker pen and mark where the bend starts and finishes.

Step 3: Start by using clean hands to gently push in the opposite direction to the bend.

Step 4: Use a disc straightening tool or an adjustable spanner to make larger adjustments.

may be because the disc rotor has been bent. Bent rotors can slow the wheels, increase brake pad wear and also make an annoying sound. Before you go out and buy a new disc it might worth attempting to straighten it. Remember, disc rotors are sharp, so be careful not to cut yourself.

Difficulty – 3/5
Time – 10 minutes

Tools
Disc straightening tool or large adjustable spanner (with flat clamping surface)
Marker pen

Step 1: Spin the wheel to locate the bend by seeing where the disc touches the brake pads in the caliper, or listen for the rubbing sound.

Step 2: Take a marker pen and mark where the bend starts to touch the brake pads and then mark where it ends. You should only mark the disc on the thin top edge of the rotor, not the braking surface.

Step 3: Rotate the bend away from the caliper and start to gently pull the disc in the opposite direction to the bend. Start by straightening the disc with your hands (ensure they are clean before you start). Spread and push your thumbs over the bend while using your fingers to push or pull against the spokes. Start with small adjustments, spin the wheel to see if it's still rubbing and make necessary corrections where needed.

Step 4: For any larger adjustments, take a disc straightening tool or a large adjustable spanner and clamp the area of the disc that is bent. Try to get the tool or spanner as far on to the disc as possible and pull away from the bend, making only small adjustments until the disc is not rubbing on the brake pads. In extreme cases you can use two adjustable spanners and pull against each spanner.

CHAPTER 10

SUSPENSION

Mountain bike suspension is not just for people who want to risk life and limb jumping off cliffs. Its real purpose is to help smooth out uneven terrain, which helps the wheels stay in contact with the ground and thus provides better grip. Suspension has existed on mountain bikes since the late 1980s and has been continuously evolving ever since. Over time suspension manufacturers have created suspension that is reliable, high performing and affordable, which in turn has pushed the boundaries of what is possible on a mountain bike.

Hardtails

Mountain bikes that have suspension on only the front forks are known as hardtails. There are a number of different types of hardtail, from lightweight carbon fibre hardtails, used for racing cross-country, through to 'hardcore hardtails', which are used for more extreme disciplines including 4X racing and freeriding.

A hardtail mountain bike.

Full Suspension

Mountain bikes that have suspension on the front and the rear are known as full suspension or full sus. Full suspension mountain bikes are also used in a variety of disciplines from cross-country to downhill racing and almost everything in between.

A full suspension mountain bike.

Suspension Terminology

Air Valves
Air-sprung suspension will have an air valve to adjust the stiffness of the suspension. You will need to use a high-pressure shock pump to adjust the pressure. To prevent the valve from leaking you should check it is tight and keep it clean.

Axle
The axle helps connect the wheels to the frame or forks. The most common is the 9mm quick release, there are many other systems but you will mainly encounter a 15mm or 20mm bolt-through on front forks.

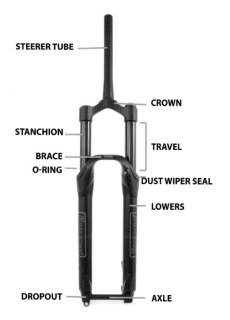

STEERER TUBE

CROWN

STANCHION

TRAVEL

BRACE

O-RING

DUST WIPER SEAL

LOWERS

DROPOUT

AXLE

Labeled diagram of forks.

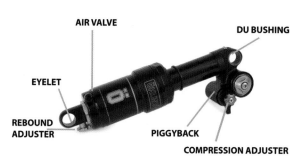

AIR VALVE

DU BUSHING

EYELET

REBOUND
ADJUSTER

PIGGYBACK

COMPRESSION ADJUSTER

Labeled diagram of rear shock.

Bushings, DU Bushings

Bushings are inserts that are used to reduce friction. They are commonly used on fork lowers and rear shock eyelets. Bushings are usually made of a soft material, usually aluminium or nylon, so they wear out before the component does.

Ensure you replace the bushings when you feel any play or movement in the bushings otherwise it could end up damaging the suspension.

Bottom-Out Bumper

A bottom out bumper is mostly used on rear shocks to cushion the shock when it fully goes through its travel after a harsh impact, also known as bottoming out.

Brace

Most forks have a brace connecting the lower fork legs together. The purpose if this is to reduce flex, which improves handling, especially in turns.

Compression Adjuster

This controls the speed of how the suspension reacts when it compresses. If there is not enough compression the suspension will run through the entire range of travel and will be likely to bottom out easily. Conversely, if there is too much compression the suspension will give a rough ride and not utilize the full travel available. Some shocks also have high- and low-speed compression adjustment, which is used to fine-tune the compression.

Crown

The crown attaches the steerer tube to the stanchions. Mountain bikes that are used for cross-country generally only have one crown, known as single crown forks, and bikes that are used for more extreme disciplines such as downhill have two crowns, known as dual crown or triple clamp forks.

Dropout

The dropout is the part of the frame or fork where the axle is mounted. Forks that are designed to be used with a 9mm quick release have a slot for the axle to sit in. Most modern forks tend to use a thicker bolt-through axle, 15mm or 20mm, which requires a hole instead of a slot on the drop out and will often feature pinch bolts or retaining bolts on the axle.

Dust Wiper Seals

There are two main types of seals: oil seals and air seals.

Oil seals, also known as 'dust wiper seals', are used to keep the lubrication/damping oil inside the suspension while keeping the dirt out. Some internal dust wiper seals also use foam rings, which absorb oil to help keep the suspension lubricated. Remember to keep dust wiper seals clean and inspect for damage on a regular basis. Air seals are generally a thinner O-ring and are used to help retain high pressures in air springs.

Eyelet

This is the 6mm or 8mm hole at either end of the rear shock. There is usually a bushing that presses into the eyelet, then mounting hardware and shock bolts are used to attach the rear shock to the frame.

Foot Nut

These bolts are positioned on the bottom of the fork lowers. They serve the important job of keeping the lower fork legs attached to the fork internals, therefore keeping the front wheel attached to the rest of the bike.

Lockout, Propedal

A lockout is a system used to block suspension action, making it rigid.

This makes climbing much more efficient as more energy goes into pedalling rather than making the suspension bob up and down. Some lockout systems have a remote control on the handlebars to make it easier to operate whilst riding.

Negative Spring

Negative springs are used to help relieve seal friction at the beginning of the travel, which is common with air-sprung suspension.

O-Ring

O-rings are used on forks and rear shocks to help measure the amount of sag when setting up the suspension.

Piggyback

Some rear shocks have an extra chamber mounted to the side of the shock called a piggyback, normally used by long travel bikes to give improved damping.

Preload Adjuster

Preload is the amount a metal spring is compressed; the more the spring is compressed, the stiffer it will be. Preload should never be used to compensate for not having the correct weight spring, so adjusting the

preload should be kept to a minimum. When adjusting the preload you may need to adjust the rebound at the same time, because more preload can make the rebound quicker.

Preload Collar

Preload collars are used on coil-sprung rear shocks; they screw against the spring to preload it. Remember, never screw more than three turns from when the preload collar comes into contact with the spring. If more preload is required, purchase a heavier spring.

Rebound Adjuster

The rebound, also known as the damping, controls the return speed of the suspension. The rebound adjuster is usually red, the more rebound (+) the faster the suspension will return, the less rebound (-) the slower it will return. To set the rebound you want to find a happy medium, so the spring does not return too fast and feel like a pogo stick, but also not too slow so the suspension cannot return to full extension fast enough, compacts down over multiple bumps and fails to operate correctly.

Lowers

The lowers are the lower cast metal or carbon fibre part of the fork that the stanchions slide into and the wheel connects into via the dropouts. It's important to inspect the lowers for damage on a regular basis.

Sag

The amount the suspension compresses under the rider's weight. A rubber O-ring normally measures this when the rider is sat on the bike.

Shock Mount, Mounting Hardware

Shock mounts are the alloy inserts that fit in between the DU bushing on the rear shock and the frame. There are many different types and sizes of shock mounts, corresponding to different frame and shock combinations. When you replace the shock mounts be sure to order the correct size, either by contacting your frame dealer or measuring the shock mount dimensions with Vernier calipers.

Spring

The spring is what makes the suspension return to full extension after a compression. They are usually made from a steel or titanium coil, or they can be a compressible chamber of air.

Stanchion

The stanchions are the slippery metal tubes that slide into the fork lowers. They range in a variety of diameters from 28mm to 40mm, the wider the diameter the stiffer and stronger they are. Stanchions are made from a variety of metals, but most commonly aluminium, which is generally coated in a special type of anodizing to reduce friction. Remember, it's important to keep your fork seals clean to prevent damage and prolong the life of the stanchions.

Steerer Tube

The steerer tube is the upper part of the fork that attaches the crown to the steering components of the bike and is generally concealed in a fully built bike. Steerer tubes come in a variety of materials, but are most commonly made from aluminium. They also range in sizes from a lightweight 1in steerer tube for endurance disciplines such as cross-country to 1.5in steerer tube for more extreme disciplines including downhill. Also, tapered steerer tubes are commonly used to get the best of both weight and strength, tapered from 1in at the top to 1.5in at the fork crown.

Travel

Suspension travel is the measurement of the range the suspension can move; this is often measured by how much the wheel axle moves when the suspension compresses. Short travel bikes, 100–150mm, are designed for disciplines such as cross-country, They require less suspension travel due to the smoother terrain and will require less bump absorption. Long travel bikes, 160–200mm+, that are used for more extreme disciplines such as downhill and freeride require more suspension travel to absorb the large bumps and impacts.

Travel Adjuster

Certain types of suspension have a feature that allows you adjust the amount of suspension travel, changing the geometry of the bike to suit the type of riding you encounter. You can reduce the amount of suspension travel for climbing, which will steepen the bike's geometry to give it better grip for steep climbs. For challenging descents you can increase the suspension travel to help absorb the bumps and also slacken the frame geometry, making it more stable at speed.

How Does Suspension Work?

All suspensions systems are based around two essential components, a spring and a damper.

The Spring

The job of the spring is to allow compression and return over bumps, keeping the wheels in contact with the ground. Modern springs are usually made from either a metal coil or a cylinder of compressed air or gas. Ideally springs should get harder the more compressed they are, known as being 'progressive'. Progressive springs are perfect for mountain bikes as they are soft enough to absorb small bumps, such as roots and rocks, while still having enough resistance to be capable of absorbing the big impacts from jumps or large drops. No matter if you have a coil or air spring, it should be set up for the rider's weight. If the spring is too soft it will make the bike hard to pedal and give an awkward ride position on the bike, but if the spring is too hard it will not absorb the bumps, causing a harsh ride.

Coil Springs

Most mountain bike coil springs are made from steel, while some of the higher end bikes may be titanium. Steel and titanium springs come in different sizes and stiffness and it is important to get the correct size and stiffness of spring that corresponds to the weight of the rider. To help find the correct spring you can use an online calculator: www.tftuned.com/spring-calculator

Steel vs. Titanium

Steel springs perform perfectly adequately for most recreational riders, but for riders and racers looking

An air spring and a coil spring.

A steel spring and a titanium spring.

to save weight and optimize performance, a titanium spring could be the best option. Titanium springs are usually between 30–50 per cent lighter than steel springs, they also hold their elasticity much longer and have also been shown to respond faster to bumps, giving better performance. The performance benefits of a titanium spring come at a price, as it costs four or five times the price of a steel spring.

Spring Fatigue

A spring wears out over time, normally resulting in it getting shorter or even breaking. As it wears out it will normally start to sag more and require more preload, which is a sign it needs replacing.

Air Spring

An air spring is a cylinder of compressed air; the more air you add the stiffer the spring will be. The advantages of an air spring is it can be easily adjusted to the rider's weight and it does not require any heavy metal coil making them much lighter. The disadvantages of an air spring are that it may not work as well on the smaller bumps and can be known to overheat on long descents.

Air or Coil

In the past, coil shocks were used for more extreme disciplines such as downhill and freeride as they give better sensitivity and performance in the first 30 per cent of the suspension travel.

Air-sprung shocks were mainly used for endurance disciplines due to the weight advantage. As air-sprung suspension technology improves people are starting to favour air springs over coils due to the adjustability and weight-saving advantage.

High- and Slow-Speed Compression

Adjusting high-speed compression affects how the suspension reacts during medium to fast movements, things like flat landings and square edge bumps.

Slow-speed compression is to finely tune how the suspension reacts during slow-speed movements, including pedalling, gentle landings and g-outs. It also affects the ride comfort and traction.

The damper.

The Damper (Rebound)

The damper, also known as the rebound, controls the return speed of the suspension. For example, if suspension had no damper, the bike would bounce all over the trail and be extremely hard to control. Most dampers work when the suspension compresses from a shock; this energy compresses a piston that forces oil through a small valve, limiting the speed at which the suspension returns.

There are two factors that control the speed of the damping: the oil viscosity, known as the weight (w/t) of the oil, and the size of the valve hole. Most suspension manufacturers will specify the weight of the oil to use with their damping system, normally you can adjust the speed of the rebound by adjusting a dial that changes the size of the hole that the oil passes through (smaller hole = slower rebound, larger hole = faster rebound). There are two main types of damper: an open bath and closed bath. Open bath dampers use oil from the inside of the fork lowers, usually requiring a large volume of oil, which dramatically increases the weight of the fork. Closed bath dampers use a cartridge, requiring a much smaller volume of oil and reducing the weight of the fork. Remember, when adding more compression or a stiffer spring, you will need to adjust the rebound slower to get the same effect.

High- and Slow-Speed Damping (Rebound)

High-speed damping can be used to stiffen up the suspension to help reduce the amount the shock bottoms out, but should never be used to compensate for not having the correct weight spring. It can also be used to soften up the end of the stroke to minimize spiking (oil build-up that cannot pass through the hole fast enough, causing a knocking noise).

Slow speed damping gives the ability to adjust how the damping reacts to small shocks. You can either make it more sensitive for things such as roots and rocks or you can make it stiffer to reduce the amount the suspension dives, or compresses, from braking.

How To: Set Up Suspension

Setting up your suspension correctly will give you a better grip, improved control and a more comfortable ride. Adjusting suspension can seem a bit daunting with all the dials and adjusters, but in fact it's very simple and won't take long to do.

How damping works

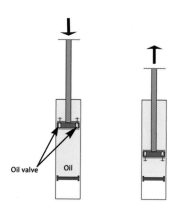

Slow-speed adjuster.

High-speed adjuster.

Setting Up Suspension Forks

Setting up your suspension correctly can make a big difference to how your bike performs; it can be the difference between holding a smooth line effortlessly down a trail or bouncing off into the spiky bushes. Most people think suspension set-up is complicated, but in fact it's a lot simpler than you may think. The two most important elements are setting the sag and rebound; the other adjustments are for fine tuning.

Difficulty – 1/5
Time – 5 minutes

Tools
Allen keys
Zip tie
Shock pump
Ruler
Riding gear

Step 1: Setting the Sag. This is adjusting how much the suspension compresses under the rider's weight. This is achieved by either adding or removing air with a shock pump or by purchasing the correct stiffness of coil spring(s).

Air Sprung

Start by sliding the rubber O-ring down to the bottom of the stanchions or to the end of the rear shock shaft, so that it is touching the outer dust seal. Gently mount the bike with both feet on the pedals, trying not to bounce on the suspension. It may help to have a friend to hold the bike stable or lean the bike again a wall. Now lightly dismount the bike without bouncing and check the O-ring to see how much suspension has compressed under your weight. As a rule, most mountain bikes should sag around 20–25 per cent (a quarter of the travel), for longer travel bikes, such as downhill bikes, it can go up to 30–35 per cent sag, but if you are unsure stick at 25 per cent.

To adjust the sag, attach a shock pump then add or remove air in 10 psi increments, paying attention to the minimum and maximum pressures that are usually printed on the fork lowers or shock body.

Slide the O-ring down to the fork's dust wiper seal. Gently mount the bike and see how much the O-ring moves.

Slide the O-ring along to the shock's dust wiper seal. Gently mount the bike and see how much the O-ring moves.

Add or remove air with a shock pump to achieve the correct amount of sag.

Setting the sag on coil-sprung suspension.

Setting the rebound.

Negative Air Springs

Some less common air forks use a negative spring, which is designed to reduce friction at the start of the fork stroke to help improve small bump sensitivity. Start by setting the negative spring at the same pressure as the positive spring; to fine tune either add more air to give a more sensitive feel or reduce the air to lessen pedal bob. Always check the minimum and maximum before you make adjustment as different brands will vary.

Coil-Sprung Suspension

To set the sag of a coil-sprung fork or rear shock you will need to have the correct spring for your weight. When you are standing on the bike without bouncing, the forks or rear shock should compress 20–25 per cent for cross-country or trail riding and 30–35 per cent for downhill or freeride. Most suspension manufacturers will have a chart on their website that can help you purchase the correct spring for your weight.

Step 2: Set the Rebound. Adjusting the rebound controls the speed the suspension decompresses, if set too fast it will bounce you down the trail and be very hard to handle, if it's set too slow it will compact down, failing to absorb bumps giving a harsh ride. So when setting the rebound you should try and find a medium between the two. To set the rebound push down firmly down on the handlebars or saddle, and quickly release, Try to add enough rebound so the wheels stays on the ground.

Step 3: Fine Tuning

Compression

Compression damping should be kept to a minimum; it's used for finely adjusting the stiffness of the suspension. More compression will make it stiffer, improving pedalling and climbing, while less will help it track the ground better, giving a more comfortable ride. Remember, if you find you need more than a few clicks/turns of compression you may need to increase the spring stiffness otherwise you could damage the damping system.

Adjusting compression damping.

High-Speed Compression

Adjusting the high-speed compression will change how the bike reacts on big impacts and fast stutter bumps. You want to find a balance of high-speed compression; not enough will give an unforgiving ride, too much will make it blow right through the suspension travel. High-speed compression is mainly used for fine tuning and can be adjusted to help the bike perform better on different types of trail.

Low-Speed Compression

Adjusting the low-speed compression controls how the bike absorbs the small bumps. You should find a balance between the two so that your suspension does not bob while pedalling, while absorbing the small bumps.

Adjusting high-speed compression.

How To: Replace DU Bushings and Shock Hardware

The rear shock is usually mounted to the bike with three main components: DU bushings, shock hardware and shock bolts.

DU Bushings

A DU bushing, also known as an eyelet bushing, is a thin cylindrical sleeve designed to protect the rear shock eyelet. If you start to notice movement in the back end of the bike it will quite likely be the DU bushing starting to wear. DU bushings are relativity cheap to replace and come in two standard sizes (12.7mm and 12mm) depending on the brand of shock. The exception to this rule is Cane Creek shocks, which come in a number of different sizes.

Adjusting low-speed compression.

12.7mm Bushing
Fox, RockShox 2004 onwards, 5th Element, Vivid, Romic, Manitou 2011 onwards, Marzocchi, Roco.

12mm Bushing
Manitou pre-2010, Xfusion.

Shock Bolts

Shock bolts usually range in sizes (normally between 6, 8 and 10mm) depending on the model and brand of frame. If you want to reduce the weight of the bike you can find aftermarket shock bolts made of titanium.

Different sized DU bushings.

A two-piece reducer.

A three-piece pin and sleeve.

A five-piece flange bushing.

Shock Hardware

The shock hardware is designed to take up the space between the DU bushing and the shock mounts on the frame. There is a wide range of sizes for shock hardware as the distance between the shock mounts varies from frame to frame and also the size of the shock.

If you do not change the DU bushing in time the shock hardware will start to wear and will need replacing at the same time. To make sure you order the correct size, use some Vernier calipers to measure the diameter of shock bolt or centre hole and the width of frame spacing, or simply measure existing shock hardware.

Types of Bushing Kits/Reducer Kits

Two-Piece Reducer
Two-piece reducer hardware that is pressed into the shock eyelet with a DU bushing.

Three-Piece Pin and Sleeve
The three-piece pin and sleeve is made up of a metal pin that is pressed through a DU bushing in the shock eyelet. There are two metal sleeves that fit over the centre pin that act as spacers.

Five-Piece Flanged Bushing
The five-piece flanged bushing is made up of two plastic flanged bushings that are pressed into the shock eyelet instead of a DU bushing. Then a hollow metal pin is pressed through the centre of the flanged bushing, followed by two spacers on either end on the metal pin to keep it centred.

Offset Bushing
Offset bushings are designed to alter the geometry of your bike. They take the place of your standard shock hardware, with the only difference being that the centre hole is offset to one side. If the offset holes are pointing towards each other it will effectively shorten the shock and slacken the head angle, lowering the bottom bracket and making the bike more stable at speed and on steeper terrain. If you have the offset holes pointing away from each other it will steepen the head angle, helping the bike grip on the climbs and making it more agile for low-speed riding. It's

An offset bushing.

important to remember that offset bushings do not change the amount of suspension travel; the stroke length will stay the same.

How To: Check Shock Bushings for Wear

Place a finger on each end of the shock bushing/hardware while gently moving the saddle up and down. If the bushings are OK you will not feel any movement or hear any knocking sounds.

If you notice any issues you will need to replace the bushing. Most frame designs will wear one end of the bushing more than the other and normally only require the worn bushing to be changed.

How To: Change a DU Bushing

When you have play in the back end of your bike it will most likely be a DU bushing. DU bushings are cheap, simple and quick to change, but more importantly doing so will get rid of that annoying play in the back end of your bike.

Difficulty – 4/5
Time – 15 minutes

Tools
Allen keys
Sockets or spanners
DU bushing tool, 12mm or 12.7mm

Vice
Straps or zip ties

Parts
DU Bushing
Shock hardware (if required)

To start you will need to remove the rear shock from the frame, remembering that once the shock is removed the frame will collapse in on its self, and if you are not careful you may stretch the gear cables, kink the brake hoses or damages paint work. So it's worth having some straps or zip ties on hand to hold the frame in position. To remove the rear shock, simply detach the mounting bolts; this will usually require an Allen key or a socket.

Step 1: Remove the shock's mounting hardware.

Step 2: Place the DU bushing tool over the bushing. Clamp the tool in a vice to push the bushing out of the shock.

147

Step 3: Place the new bushing on the tool and use a vice to press the bushing in. Ensure the bushing goes in straight; if necessary, start again.

Step 4: Press the mounting hardware into the shock eyelet and fit the shock back onto the frame.

Step 1: Remove the shock hardware. If the shock hardware or DU bushing is well worn the hardware may just fall out or pull out by hand, otherwise place the shock hardware in a vice with soft jaws and gently pull it loose.

Step 2: Split the DU bushing tool. Put one half of the tool either side of the shock eyelet, making sure the driving part is lined up over the DU bushing, then place in a vice and clamp the tool together until the DU bushing is fully removed.

Step 3: Place the new DU bushing over the driving part of the DU bushing tool; some tools have a recess to slot on the new bushing. Slowly clamp up the tool and bush in the vice, ensuring you keep it all straight.

Press the bushing in by clamping the vice against the tool until the bushing is flush with both sides of the shock.

Step 4: Reinstall the shock hardware, which may push in by hand or you may need to press them in with the vice. Now remount the shock back on to the frame. If you have a torque wrench check the necessary torque settings, which are often marked on the frame or in the owner's manual.

How To: Service Fox Forks

Keeping your suspension forks well maintained will help them stay running smooth and dramatically improve their lifespan. The procedure in this tutorial should be carried out about every thirty hours of riding, hence it's known as the thirty-hour service, but it will be referred to here as a lower leg service. This process with be similar for most Fox forks, but remember to always check the manufacturer's instructions before starting the service. For other makes of forks the process is likely to be very similar, but you will need to check the manufacturer's instructions.

If you notice your forks are leaving an oily residue on the fork stanchions, this will be a good indication that your dust wiper seals need replacing. Remember to purchase the correct dust wiper seals for your forks; this will be specific to the brand, model and year.

Difficulty – 4/5
Time – 40 Minutes

Tools
Allen keys
Socket set
Mallet
Shock pump
Pick
18mm spanner (dust seal replacement only)
Large syringe (with measurements marked on) or measuring jug and thin noised funnel
Drip pan/bucket
Seal driver (size depending on seal size, tool optional)
Latex gloves

Parts
Dust seals (if needed)
Degreaser
Paper towels or clean rag
Fox float fluid
Suspension grease
Fork oil (weight and volume depending on year and model of fork)

To make the process easier, start by removing the forks from the bike, although if you are in a hurry you can rest the bike upside down on the handlebars and saddle. If unsure of how to remove the forks *see* Chapter 7: How To: Remove and Install a Threadless Headset.

Step 1: Clamp the forks' steerer tube securely on to the bike stand. If servicing an air fork, unscrew the blue top cap and attach a shock pump. Take note of the pressure and then decompress all the air with the button on the pump.

Step 2: Remove any compression or rebound adjusters on the bottom of the fork legs. This may often require the use of a 2mm or 2.5mm Allen key. Some adjusters often have a small ball bearing inside, so slowly remove the adjuster and put it somewhere safe.

Step 3: There will be a foot nut on the bottom of each leg. Find the corresponding socket size and unscrew the nuts until they protrude from the silver internal threads by 2–3mm. Place a drip pan on the floor under the forks to catch any oil. Take a mallet and tap each foot nut with a socket until the internals are free from the lowers. Now fully unscrew the foot nuts, pull off the crush washers and slide the lowers apart from the stanchions. Hold both the lowers and stanchions over the drip pan and allow any excess oil to drip away. Take a paper towel and wipe the stanchions and lowers free of any oil.

Step 4: Spray the inside of the fork lowers with a degreaser while holding them over the drip pan. Ideally, use an alcohol-based brake cleaner because it should not leave any residue. Wrap a long thin object

Step 1: Secure the fork's steerer tube to a bike stand. Attach a shock pump, note down the pressure and decompress all the air.

Step 2: Remove any adjusters on the bottom of the fork legs.

Step 3a: Unscrew the foot nut two or three turns.

149

SUSPENSION

Step 3b: Tap the socket on the foot nut to release the stanchion from the lowers.

Step 4: Clean the fork lowers and stanchion with a degreaser.

Step 3c: Once free, remove the foot nuts and pull the stanchions apart from the lowers over a bucket to catch the oil.

Step 5: Remove and clean the foam rings. Then leave them to soak in fork oil or Fox float fluid.

Step 3d: Wipe off excess oil.

Step 6a: Line seals with suspension grease.

such as an Allen key or a screwdriver with a rag and slide it up and down both sides of the lower legs, attempting to remove as much oil and dirt as possible. If reusing the dust wiper seals, make sure the inside of the seal is fully clean.

Step 5: Remove the foam rings, which are located under the dust wiper seals. Either use a pick or often they can be pulled out with your fingers. Spray the foam rings with disc brake cleaner and use a paper towel to absorb any excess dirt/oil. Fill a small container with any fork oil, drop in the foam rings and leave for a few minutes to soak. Then refit the foam rings under the dust wiper seals.

Step 6: Line the inside of the dust wiper seals with a thin layer of suspension grease and slide the stanchions through the seals, while keeping the foot nut rods still inside the lower legs. Be careful not to pinch the seal or the sprung silver O-rings.

Step 7: Measure out the correct weight and volume of suspension oil with either a syringe or a measuring jug. For oil weights and volumes see the suspension manufacturer's website.

Turn the fork upside down and use a syringe or funnel to pour the oil into the hole of the corresponding leg.

Step 8: Push the stanchions into the fork lowers until the threaded rod pokes through the hole in the bottom of the lowers. Replace the crush washer (if fitting new dust wiper seals there will be new crush washers in the pack). Reinstall the foot nuts. Refit any adjustment dials that were connected under the foot nuts.

Step 9: Turn the forks the right way up. For air forks connect a shock pump, set to the correct pressure, and replace the blue top cap. If applicable, refit the forks back on to the bike, remembering to tighten the stem bolts to the correct torque setting. Finish by compressing the fork ten to fifteen times and wipe away any excess oil or grease off the stanchions.

Step 6b: Carefully slide the stanchions into the dust wiper seals.

Step 7a: Measure out the correct volume of lubrication oil.

Step 7b: Turn the forks upside down and put the correct volume of oil into the appropriate leg.

Step 8a: Push the stanchions fully down into the fork lowers until the silver thread sticks out.

Step 8b: Refit the crush washer and fasten the foot nut. Reattach any adjusters.

Step 9: Connect the shock pump and reset pressure. Finish by wiping off any excess oil.

How To: Service a Fox Air Rear Shock

The thought of opening up and servicing a rear shock might seem a little challenging at first, but in fact you will be amazed how quick and simple is the process. If you ride your bike a lot it's worth servicing your rear shock every two to three months; this will help improve the shock's performance and also increase its longevity. This tutorial is a Fox Float Air rear shock and although the process shown will be similar for most other air shocks, you should always check the manufacturer's guidelines before servicing your own.

Difficulty – 4/5
Time – 40 Minutes

Tools
Allen keys
Pic
Shock pump
Vice (with soft jaws)
Latex gloves
Safety glasses

Parts
Fox float fluid
Suspension grease
Isopropyl alcohol or brake cleaner
Paper towel or clean rag

Step 1: Start by taking the shock off the bike; this usually just involves removing Allen key bolts from each end of the shock. Remove any shock hardware located below the shock's shaft. If the hardware does not pull out by hand you may need to hold the hardware in a soft-jawed vice or press out with a socket.

Step 2: Check there is no trapped air causing the shock to stick down, otherwise dismantling could cause injury. Simply measure the distance between the shock mounting bolts and compare against the manufacturer's specifications. If it appears to be stuck down, send it off to a suspension service centre.

Step 3: Once you are sure the shock is the correct

Step 1: Remove shock from the frame and remove any shock hardware.

length connect a shock pump to the valve on the shock and take note of the pressure. Fully release all the air from the shock with the button on the pump or with the end of an Allen key.

Step 4: Put on your safety glasses and clamp the shock securely in the vice. Some shocks have a silver C-clip to retain the air can; if so remove the C-clip with a blunt pick or an old spoke. Now fully unscrew the air sleeve anticlockwise by hand; once free pull away from the shock and place to one side.

Step 5: Spray the air sleeve and main shock shaft with Isopropyl alcohol or brake cleaner and then wipe clean, ensuring the shock is free from oil or debris.

Step 2: Check the length of the shock to ensure it is not stuck down.

Step 4: If necessary, remove the C-clip and unscrew the air can.

Step 3: Fully release all the air from the shock with a shock pump or an Allen key.

Step 5: Clean the inside of the shock with disc brake cleaner. Ensure the shock is free from oil and debris.

Step 6: Apply a thin layer of suspension grease to the seals and then slide back onto the shock body.

Step 7: Put the shock upright in a vice and apply 4cc of Fox float fluid for lubrication.

Step 6: Apply a thin layer of suspension grease to all the seals and then slide the air sleeve back on to the main shock body.

Step 7: Clamp the shock upright in the vice and add 4cc of fox float fluid to the inside of the shock; this will help keep it lubricated.

Step 8: Turn the rebound adjuster to the fully closed position; this will help relieve some of the negative pressure while reconnecting the threads on the air sleeve. Push the shock together while twisting the air sleeve clockwise. Screw on the air sleeve until it is tight, remembering that the air sleeve only needs to be done up hand tight.

Step 9: If required, refit the C-clip to retain the air sleeve. Repressurize the shock to the correct pressure and refit the shock to the bike, remembering to use manufacturer's torque settings.

Step 8: Twist the rebound adjuster to fully closed position. Then compress the shock together while twisting until tight.

Step 9: Replace any retaining C-clips. Refit shock hardware. Set the shock to the correct pressure, and mount to the frame.

GLOSSARY

Bleed   Removing air from fluid.

Chain suck   When the chain does not release from the bottom of the chainring and jams.

Cleat   A piece of metal connected under the shoe that clips in and out of clipless pedals.

Clipless pedals   A pedal that has a mechanism allowing the rider's shoes to be connected to the bike.

DH   Downhill

Drivetrain   The components that allow the bike to be propelled: pedals, cranks, chainrings, chain, cassette and derailleur.

Enduro   A discipline of mountain bike racing where riders ride up and are timed on multiple downhill stages.

Flat pedal   Normal pedals usually with pins for grip and no mechanism into which to clip.

Full suspension   Suspension on both the frame and the forks.

Gear ratio   The combination of cogs on the cassette, chainring or a combination of them both.

Hardtail   Suspension only on the front forks.

Head angle   The angle at which the frames head tube is positioned.

Maxle   A quick release, bolt-through axle.

Nipple   Nipples screw on to the end of spokes, attaching the spoke to the rim.

PSI   A measurement of pressure (pounds per square inch).

Presta   A thin inner tube or tubeless valve.

Rebound   The speed at which suspension decompresses.

Sag   The amount suspension compresses with the rider's weight.

Schrader   An inner tube valve also commonly found on car wheels.

Shock pump   High-pressure pump used to adjust air pressure on suspension.

Snakebite   A type of puncture with two holes in close proximity.

Star nut   A nut that is pressed into a fork's steerer tube, allowing the headset to be tightened against the stem.

Steerer tube   The steerer tube attaches the fork's crown to the handlebars.

Tyre tread   The pattern of rubber on a tyre.

Torque   A measurement of force used to tighten components to the correct tension.

Torx   A six-pointed, star-shaped pattern used on bolt heads that requires a compatible key.

Travel   The amount suspension compresses.

Tubeless   Tyres that do not require an inner tube.

Wheelbase   The measurements from the back of the chain stay to the front axle.

XC   Cross-country.

APPENDIX

CONVERSION TABLES

Mountain bike components come from all over the world, which means different brands will use different units of measurement. The following conversion tables should help convert the most common units of measure.

Centimetres (cm) to Inches (inch)

Centimetre and inches are commonly used for measuring frame geometry, handlebar width and suspension travel.

Pound Per Square Inch (PSI) to Bar

PSI and bar, measurements of pressure, are commonly used for tyre pressure and air-sprung suspension.

Centimetres (cm)	Inches (in) (decimal)
1	0.39
2	0.78
2.54	1.00
3	1.18
4	1.57
5	1.96
6	2.36
7	2.75
8	3.14
9	3.54
10	3.93
20	7.87
30	11.81
40	15.78
50	19.68
60	23.62
70	27.55
80	31.49
90	35.43
100	39.37

Psi	Bar	Psi	Bar	Psi	Bar
1	0.068	26	1.792	51	3.516
2	0.137	27	1.861	52	3.585
3	0.206	28	1.930	53	3.654
4	0.275	29	1.999	54	3.723
5	0.344	30	2.068	55	3.792
6	0.413	31	2.137	56	3.861
7	0.482	32	2.206	57	3.930
8	0.551	33	2.275	58	3.998
9	0.620	34	2.344	59	4.067
10	0.689	35	2.413	60	4.136
11	0.758	36	2.482	61	4.205
12	0.827	37	2.551	62	4.274
13	0.896	38	2.620	63	4.343
14	0.965	39	2.688	64	4.412
15	1.034	40	2.757	65	4.481
16	1.103	41	2.826	66	4.550
17	1.172	42	2.895	67	4.619
18	1.241	43	2.964	68	4.688
19	1.310	44	3.033	69	4.757
20	1.378	45	3.102	70	4.826
21	1.447	46	3.171	71	4.895
22	1.516	47	3.240	72	4.964
23	1.585	48	3.309	73	5.033
24	1.654	49	3.378	74	5.102
25	1.723	50	3.447	75	5.171

Millilitres to Fluid Ounces

Millilitres and fluid ounces are commonly used for measuring brake and suspension fluid.

Millilitres (ml)	US Fluid Ounces (fl oz)
1	0.03
10	0.34
20	0.68
30	1.01
40	1.35
50	1.69
60	2.03
70	2.37
80	2.71
90	3.04
100	3.38
200	6.76
300	10.14
400	13.52
500	16.90
600	20.28
700	23.67
800	27.05
900	30.43
1,000 (1 Litre)	33.81

INDEX